PELICAN BOOKS

AN OUTLINE OF
EUROPEAN ARCHITECTURE

BY

NIKOLAUS PEVSNER

(A 109)

Lucy Imbach

THE AUTHOR

BORN in 1902, Dr. Nikolaus Pevsner is married and has three children. Is a Lecturer in Art at Birkbeck College (University of London); Editor of the King Penguin Books; Assistant Editor of *The Architectural Review*, and one of the most learned and stimulating writers on art in England.

Has studied the history of art and architecture in Germany; was five years on the staff of the Dresden Gallery; four years lecturer at Göttingen University, where he specialised in the History of Art in Great Britain.

Has written the standard work on *Italian Painting of Mannerism and Baroque*, also *Pioneers of the Modern Movement (from William Morris to Walter Gropius)*, *An Enquiry into Industrial Art in England*, and *Academies of Art, Past and Present*.

PELICAN BOOKS

AN OUTLINE OF
EUROPEAN ARCHITECTURE

BY

NIKOLAUS PEVSNER

Revised and enlarged edition

PUBLISHED BY

PENGUIN BOOKS

HARMONDSWORTH MIDDLESEX ENGLAND

245 FIFTH AVENUE   NEW YORK   U.S.A.

First published March 1943
Revised and enlarged edition 1945

This little book I dedicate to you,
my three children, in East, North
and West, hoping that, when you are
grown up, the world will once again
be safe for studying and enjoying
the achievements of all nations

MADE AND PRINTED IN GREAT BRITAIN FOR PENGUIN BOOKS LIMITED
BY RICHARD CLAY AND COMPANY, LTD., BUNGAY, SUFFOLK

COLLOGRAVURE PLATES PRINTED IN GREAT BRITAIN BY HARRISON AND SONS LTD.
44–47, ST. MARTIN'S LANE, LONDON, W.C.2, PRINTERS TO H.M. THE KING

CONTENTS

ILLUSTRATIONS

vi

(b) Photogravure Plates

ACKNOWLEDGEMENTS

THE author wishes to express his thanks to the following for permission to reproduce photographs and drawings: The Architectural Press, Ltd. (figs. 22 and 50); Messrs. B. T. Batsford, Ltd. (plate XVIII, figs. 20, 21, 23 and 44); Professor K. C. Conant (plate VII B and fig. 6); Country Life, Ltd. (plates XLIII B, XLIV B); Mr. H. Felton (plate XX A); The Sir John Soane Museum (plate XLV A).

FOREWORD TO THE FIRST EDITION

A HISTORY of European architecture to the dimensions dictated by the format of this series can achieve its goal only if the reader is prepared to concede three things.

He must not expect to find a mention of every work and every architect of importance. If this had been attempted, the space available would would have been filled with nothing but names of architects, names of buildings, and dates. One building must be accepted as sufficient to illustrate one particular style or one particular point. This means that in the picture which the reader is going to see gradations are eliminated, and colour is set against colour. He may regard that as a disadvantage, but he will, it can be hoped, admit that the introduction of subtler differences would have doubled or trebled the bulk of the book. Thus the nave of Lincoln will be discussed but not the nave of Wells, and Sto. Spirito in Florence but not S. Lorenzo. Whether St. Michael's, Coventry, is really a more complete or suitable example of a Perpendicular parish church than Holy Trinity, Hull, the Palazzo Rucellai of the Italian Renaissance than the Palazzo Strozzi, is of course debatable. Unanimity cannot be achieved on matters of that kind. Yet, as architectural values can be appreciated only by describing and analysing buildings at some length, it was imperative to cut down their number, and devote as much space as possible to those finally retained.

Besides this limitation, two more have proved necessary. It was out of the question to treat European architecture of all ages from Stonehenge to the 20th century, or the architecture of all the nations which make up Europe to-day. Neither would however be expected of a volume called European architecture. The Greek temple, most readers probably feel, belongs to the civilisation of Antiquity, not to what we usually mean when we talk of European civilisation. It will also be agreed, though for quite different reasons, that the architecture of, say, Bulgaria need not be

dealt with in these pages. The main reasons here are that
Bulgaria in the past belonged to the Byzantine and then to
the Russian orbit, and that her importance now is so
marginal as to make her omission pardonable. So everything will be left out of this book that is only of marginal
interest in the development of European architecture, and
everything that is not European or—as I thus propose using
the term European—Western in character. For Western
civilisation is a distinct unit, a biological unit, one is tempted
to say. Not for racial reasons certainly—it is shallow
materialism to assume that—but for cultural reasons.
Which nations make up Western civilisation at any given
moment, at what juncture a nation enters it, at what juncture
a nation ceases to be of it—such questions are for the
individual historian to decide. Nor can he expect his
decision to be universally accepted. The cause of this
uncertainty regarding historical categories is obvious enough.
Though a civilisation may appear entirely clear in its essential characteristics when we think of its highest achievements, it seems blurred and hazy when we try to focus
its exact outlines in time and space.

Taking Western civilisation, it is certain that prehistory
is not part of it, as the prehistory of every civilisation—the
word expresses it—is a stage *prae*, i.e., before that civilisation
itself is born. The birth of a civilisation coincides with the
moment when a leading idea, a *leitmotiv*, emerges for the
first time, the idea which will in the course of the centuries
to follow gather strength, spread, mature, mellow, and
ultimately—this is fate, and must be faced—abandon the
civilisation whose soul it had been. When this happens,
the civilisation dies, and another, somewhere else or from
the same soil, grows up, starting out of its own prehistory
into its own primitive dark age, and then developing its
own essentially new ideology. Thus it was, to recall only
the most familiar example, when the Roman Empire died,
and Western civilisation was born out of prehistoric
darkness, passed through its Merovingian infancy, and then
took shape first under Charlemagne and finally during the
reign of Otto the Great in the 10th century.

Now, besides prehistory and Antiquity, nearly all that

FOREWORD TO THE SECOND EDITION

THERE is one considerable difference between the previous edition and this. The publisher has found it possible to add sixteen plates to the thirty-two originally printed. This has enabled me to fill in the worst gaps in the illustrations. While thus the total of pictures has gone up from 107 to 146, the length of the text differs between the two editions only by 72 pages. This is as it should be. For although I had tried in the first edition to put as little as possible into the text without corresponding documentation in the pictures and although reviewers of the book had appreciated this apparently unusual attitude and been extremely kind to the book and to me, I was sorely aware of the fact that it had in a good many cases been impossible for me to provide a sufficient visual backing for my arguments. Not all these cases are eliminated now, but most of them and, I hope, the relevant ones.

The most serious omission in the original text was Spain. I had decided, after much hesitation, to leave it out, partly for lack of space, and partly because I have never travelled in Spain. Then however Geoffrey Webb in his very generous review in *The Architectural Review* brought forward such incontrovertible reasons for giving Spain her due, even in the smallest of histories of architecture, that I changed my mind and said what little I could on the Visigothic-" Carolingian " style, the Late Gothic of the 15th century, the Plateresque, and the 18th-century Baroque. All these expressions of the Spanish character in architecture may, from the European point of view, not be as central as events in France and Italy, but they are not more marginal than, say, the Elizabethan style in England or the Rococo in Germany.

Regarding other additions, as it may be tedious to anybody conversant with the first edition to search for them, I will give here a list of most of them. Page 40 has a little more on the schools of French Romanesque than there had belongs to the first one thousand years A.D. has had to be left out, because the events of that age, centred in the Eastern Mediterranean—i.e., the orientalisation of the Roman Empire, early Christianity, early Talmudism, early Mohammedanism and the Byzantine Empire, with its successor civilisations in the Balkans and Russia—make up a separate civilisation of its own, of a character fundamentally different from the Greek and Roman as well as the Western.

So these three omissions—all omissions in time—will, it is to be hoped, be considered justifiable.   As for limitations in space, a few words will suffice.   Whoever makes up his mind to write a short history of European architecture, or art, or philosophy, or drama, or agriculture, must decide in which part of Europe at any time those things happened which seem to him to express most intensely the vital will and vital feelings of Europe.   It is for this reason that e.g. Germany is not mentioned for her 16th-century but for her 18th-century buildings, and Spain not for her rôle in the history of Western Mohammedan but exclusively of Western Christian architecture, that buildings in the Netherlands are only touched upon, and Scandinavian buildings not mentioned at all.   The only positive bias towards the work of one nation that has been permitted (and needs no special apology) is towards British examples where they could be introduced, without obscuring the issue, instead of examples from abroad.   The issue, to say it once more, is Western architecture as an expression of Western civilisation, described historically in its growth from the 9th to the 19th century.

The author wishes cordially to thank Margaret Whinney and Anthony Blunt for reading his text in typescript and improving it in many ways.

LONDON, January 1942

INTRODUCTION

A BICYCLE shed is a building; Lincoln Cathedral is a piece of architecture. Nearly everything that encloses space on a scale sufficient for a human being to move in, is a building; the term architecture applies only to buildings designed with a view to æsthetic appeal. Now æsthetic sensations may be caused by a building in three different ways. First, they may be produced by the treatment of walls, proportions of windows, the relation of wall-space to window-space, of one story to another, of ornamentation such as the tracery of a 14th-century window, or the leaf and fruit garlands of a Wren porch. Secondly, the treatment of the exterior of a building as a whole is æsthetically significant, its contrasts of block against block, the effect of a pitched or a flat roof or a dome, the rhythm of projections and recessions. Thirdly, there is the effect on our senses of the treatment of the interior, the sequence of rooms, the widening out of a nave at the crossing, the stately movement of a baroque staircase. The first of these three ways is two-dimensional; it is the painter's way. The second is three-dimensional, and as it treats the building as volume, as a plastic unit, it is the sculptor's way. The third is three-dimensional too, but it concerns space; it is the architect's own way more than the others. What distinguishes architecture from painting and sculpture is its spatial quality. In this, and only in this, no other artist can emulate the architect. Thus the history of architecture is primarily a history of man shaping space, and the historian must keep spatial problems always in the foreground. This is why no book on architecture, however popular its presentation may be, can be successful without ground-plans.

But architecture, though primarily spatial, is not exclusively spatial. In every building, besides enclosing space, the architect models volume and plans surface, i.e., designs an exterior and sets out individual walls. That means that the good architect requires the sculptor's and the painter's been. From page 66 to 89 nearly all is new, a somewhat more comprehensive analysis of Decorated and Perpendicular in England, the Late Gothic of the Friars and of Spain, and the " Sondergotik " of Germany. Pages 109 to about 120 contain an all-too-brief account of Mannerism in Italian architecture, a style which has proved—and for topical reasons—to be of a very special interest to the younger art historians during the last twenty years. I have given a somewhat more detailed account of it in the first volume of *The Mint* (Routledge, 1945). Pages 151 to 153 have a note on the development of staircases in the 16th and 17th centuries. The note on page 123 of the first edition was wrong, and needed revision. On pages 163 to 165 some new matter, though not enough, will be found on the Elizabethan and Jacobean styles. Pages 187 to 189 are given to some hints on the landscape garden, one of the greatest English contributions to Western architecture, and one treated quite inadequately in the first edition. Finally on pages 191 to 202 comment on the Classical and the early Gothic Revival is amplified and some lines of appreciation inserted on the genius of John Soane and Friedrich Gilly.

LONDON, March 1945

modes of vision in addition to his own spatial imagination. Thus architecture is the most comprehensive of all visual arts and has a right to claim superiority over the others.

This æsthetic superiority is, moreover, supplemented by a social superiority. Neither sculpture nor painting, although both are rooted in elementary creative and imitative instincts, surround us to the same extent as architecture, act upon us so incessantly and so ubiquitously. We can avoid intercourse with what people call the Fine Arts, but we cannot escape buildings and the subtle but penetrating effects of their character, noble, or mean, restrained or ostentatious, genuine or meretricious. An age without painting is conceivable, though no believer in the life-enhancing function of art would want it. An age without easel-pictures can be conceived without any difficulty, and, thinking of the predominance of easel-pictures in the 19th century, might be regarded as a consummation devoutly to be wished. An age without architecture is impossible as long as human beings populate this world.

The very fact that in the 19th century easel-painting flourished at the expense of wall-painting and ultimately of architecture, proves into what a diseased state the arts (and Western civilisation) had fallen. The very fact that the Fine Arts to-day seem to be recovering their architectural character makes one look into the future with some hope. For architecture did rule when Greek art and when mediæval art grew and were at their best; Raphael still and Michelangelo conceived in terms of balance between architecture and painting. Titian did not, Rembrandt did not, nor did Velasquez. Very high æsthetic achievements are possible in easel-painting, but they are achievements torn out of the common ground of life. The 19th century and, even more forcibly, some of the most recent tendencies in the fine arts have shown up the dangers of the take-it-or-leave-it attitude of the independent, self-sufficient painter. Salvation can only come from architecture as the art most closely bound up with the necessities of life, with immediate use, and functional and structural fundamentals.

That does not, however, mean that architectural evolution is caused by function and construction. A style in art belongs to the world of mind, not the world of matter. New purposes may result in new types of building, but the architect's job is to make such new types both æsthetically and functionally satisfactory—and not all ages have considered, as ours does, functional soundness indispensable for æsthetic enjoyment. The position is similar with regard to materials. New materials may make new forms possible, and even call for new forms. Hence it is quite justifiable, if so many works on architecture (especially in England) have emphasized their importance. If in this book they have deliberately been kept in the background, the reason is that materials can become architecturally effective only when the architect instils into them an æsthetic meaning. Architecture is not the product of materials and purposes—nor by the way of social conditions—but of the changing spirits of changing ages. It is the spirit of an age that pervades its social life, its religion, its scholarship and its arts. The Gothic style was not created because somebody invented rib-vaulting. The Gothic spirit existed and expressed itself in rib-vaults, as has been proved and will be mentioned again later, before the constructional possibilities of the rib had been discovered. The Modern Movement did not come into being because steel frame and reinforced concrete construction had been worked out—they were worked out because a new spirit required them.

Thus the following chapters will treat the history of European architecture as a history of expression, and primarily of spatial expression.

CHAPTER ONE

TWILIGHT AND DAWN

(FROM THE 6TH TO THE 10TH CENTURIES)

THE Greek temple is the most perfect example ever achieved of architecture finding its fulfilment in bodily beauty. Its interior mattered infinitely less than its exterior. The colonnade all round conceals where the entrance lies. The faithful did not enter it and spend hours of communication with the Divine in it, as they do in a church. Our Western conception of space would have been just as unintelligible to a man of Pericles's age as our religion. It is the plastic shape of the temple that tells, placed before us with a physical presence more intense, more alive than that of any later building. The isolation of the Parthenon or the temples of Paestum, clearly disconnected from the ground on which they stand, the columns with their resilient curves, strong enough to carry without too much visible effort the weight of the architraves, the sculptured friezes and sculptured pediments—there is something consummately human in all this, life in the brightest light of nature and mind: nothing harrowing, nothing problematic and obscure, nothing blurred.

Roman architecture of the age of Augustus adopted this attitude to building, although with characteristic modifications due to the active engineering minds of the Romans. Then, however, during the 2nd and 3rd centuries a fundamental change of spirit and no longer only of forms took place. The relative stability of the Roman Empire was overthrown after the death of Marcus Aurelius (180); rulers followed each other at a rate such as had been known only during short periods of civil war. Between Marcus Aurelius and Constantine, in 125 years, there were forty-seven emperors; less than four years was the average duration of a reign. They were no longer elected by the Roman Senate, that enlightened body of politically experienced citizens, but proclaimed by some provincial army of barbarian troops, often barbarians themselves, rude soldiers of peasant stock, ignorant of and unsympathetic to the achievements of Roman civilisation. There was constant internecine warfare, and constant attacks of barbarians from outside had to be repulsed. Cities declined and were in the end deserted, their market halls and baths and blocks of flats collapsed. Soldiers of the Roman army sacked Roman towns. Goths, Alamans, Franks, Persians sacked whole provinces. Trade, seaborne and landborne, came to an end, estates and farms and villages became self-supporting once again, payments in money were replaced by payments in kind; taxes were often paid in kind. The educated bourgeoisie decimated by wars, executions, murder, and a lower and lower birthrate had no longer a share in public affairs. Men from Syria, Asia Minor, Egypt, from Spain, Gaul and Germany, held all the important positions. The subtle political balance of the Early Empire could no longer be appreciated and was no longer maintained.

When a new stability was brought about by Diocletian and Constantine about 300, it was the stability of an Oriental autocracy with a rigid oriental court ceremonial, with a merciless army and far-reaching State control. Soon Rome was no longer the capital of the Empire; Constantinople took her place. Then the Empire fell into two: that of the East to prove mighty, that of the West to become the prey of Teutonic invaders, the Visigoths, the Vandals, the Ostrogoths, the Lombards, and then for a while to be part of the Eastern—the Byzantine—Empire.

Now during these centuries the vast complexes of the late Roman palaces, baths, markets were built with their massive walls, arches, vaults, apses and niches and their inflated decoration. The Eastern Mediterranean, Egypt, Syria, Asia Minor, Palmyra, was the leader in this new style, which is in fact the direct successor to the Hellenistic style of 200 and 100 B.C.

The Eastern Mediterranean led in matters of the spirit too. From the East came the new attitude towards religion. Men were tired of what human intellect could provide. The invisible, the mysterious, the irrational were the need of that orientalised, barbarised population. The various creeds of the Gnostics, Mithraism from Persia, Judaism, Manichaeism, found their followers. Christianity proved strongest, found lasting forms of organisation, and survived the danger under Constantine of an alliance with the Empire. But it remained Eastern in essence. Tertullian's: " I believe in it because it is absurd " would have been an impossible tenet for an enlightened Roman. Augustine's " Beauty cannot be beheld in any bodily matter " is equally anti-antique. Of the greatest of the late Pagan philosophers, Plotinus, his pupil and biographer said that he walked like one ashamed of being in the body. Plotinus came from Egypt, St. Augustine from Libya. St. Athanasius and Origen were Egyptians; Basil was born and lived in Asia Minor, Diocletian was a native of Dalmatia, Constantine's father, St. Jerome and also the Emperor had grown up in the Hungarian plains. Judged by the standards of the age of Augustus, none of them was a Roman.

Their architecture represents them, their fanaticism and their passionate search for the invisible, the magic, the immaterial. S. Apollinare Nuovo in Ravena (pl. 1) was built early in the 6th century by Theodoric, ruler of the Ostrogoths in Italy. Yet there is nothing specifically Teutonic in it; it belongs wholly to that universal but, in its essentials, Eastern style that goes under the name of Early Christian. The functional elements of a Christian church are here already so completely established that neither a Gothic nor a present-day church have gone beyond it. The type is that known as the basilica, derived from halls in Late Roman palaces, though not, it seems, from any one kind in particular. The church is taken as the visible symbol of the way of the faithful towards the mystery of the Real Presence. The altar under the apse and the miracle of the Real Presence are the goal. The transept may be a halt placed between the nave and the apse. The nave with its uninterrupted sequence of columns dividing off the aisles, draws us irresistibly on towards the East. There is no articulation in that long colonnade to arrest our eyes, nor in the long row of window after window up in the clerestory; and the solemn and silent mosaic figures of martyrs and holy virgins, with their motionless faces and stiff garments, march with us.

One monotonous mesmerising rhythm fills the whole of the church—no secondary motifs weaken its fanatical single-mindedness.

Yet there is nothing primitive and barbaric in that southern art of the 6th century. That distinguishes it from all contemporary art north of the Alps. The means employed for achieving the architectural expression desired are sometimes so complex and sophisticated that only men of

Fig. 1.—Ravenna: S. Vitale, completed 547. Inner width of octagon *c.* 120 ft.

high sensibility could conceive and appreciate them. This applies especially to centrally planned churches such as Sta. Sophia in Constantinople, the greatest work of Byzantine architecture (532-37) and in Italy S. Vitale in Ravenna (completed in 547), both built by Justinian, who had made Ravenna his Italian capital after the fall of the Ostrogoths. S. Vitale (pl. II A and fig. 1) is an octagon with a two-storeyed octagonal ambulatory, a chancel and apse added at the East end, and at the West end a narthex or anteroom for the congregation to collect before entering the House of God. The spatial motif that determines the character of the room, a motif of purely æsthetic, i.e., no functional purpose, is the use of the niches into which the central octagon expands. As these niches are not enclosed by walls, but open out with arcades into the ambulatories on the ground floor and the first floor, no clear distinction exists between the two main parts of the building. The central space flows into the ambulatory, and the ambulatory becomes a senseless shape if looked at as an independent unit. The same sensation of uncertainty, of a dreamlike floating, is created, where solid walls remain, by the mosaics covering them. These glowing surfaces with austere, gaunt figures in sombre tints, seem just as immaterial, as magical and weightless 'as the surging and drooping curves of the octagon.

The Franks in Gaul, the Angles and Saxons in Britain, the Visigoths in Spain could not possibly appreciate the subtle mysteries of such churches. Theirs was still the outlook of native tribes, although Chlodovec had accepted in 496 what he understood as Christianity. With the same merciless cruelty in which the Anglo-Saxon warrior revelled in England, all but exterminating what had remained of civilisation on the island, the princes of the Merovingians sought to exterminate whole families of rivals. The pages of Gregory of Tours, who wrote in the second half of the 6th century, are full of assassination, rape and perjury. Yet this is how our own civilisation began, and how all civilisations begin—in the darkness of tribal barbarism. The Church was the only tie between these shifting kingdoms and the spiritual achievements of the South. Thus Anglo-Saxon brutality was tamed by Irish monasticism (inspired in some obscure way by the Coptic Church of Egypt) in the North and by missionaries from Rome in the South, until, early in the 8th century, the Venerable Bede and the circle around him attained a height of education unparalleled anywhere else in Europe. What they built seems primitive to us, a much simplified imitation of the Early Christian basilica, such as Brixworth, or simpler still, long naves and chancels in rude masonry without aisles. It may however well be, as descriptions seem to indicate, that large churches, such as York Cathedral, reflected more faithfully early Italian magnificence. The position was similar amongst the Franks even at the time of Charlemagne. He had grown up illiterate; he never wrote with ease. But he had a conscious programme of educating his people or peoples to a conception of Roman urbanity and Roman grandeur in a new Christian guise. Hence he gathered round his person the flower of European scholarship and poetry, men from England, Spain, France and Italy—all ecclesiastics, of course. Hence he built for himself palaces with hall, chapel and large ranges of rooms, all as clearly organised in their

← Chapel with apse, two square vestries and screen between choir and nave.

← Courtyard with arcades.

Domestic building with colonnade → in front.

← Imperial Hall with apse.

Fig. 2.—Ingelheim: Charlemagne's Palace, early 9th century.

relative positions as the palaces of the Roman Emperors on the Palatine, and all connected by vast colonnades of evidently Roman Eastern derivation (fig. 2). Hence his inspiration for the plans of some of the greatest of his churches—e.g., St. Denis and Fulda—came from the Constantinian Rome of old St. Peter's, i.e., the glory of Christian-Imperial Rome. And hence, on Christmas Day of the year 800, he made the Pope crown him in Rome with the crown of a new Holy Roman Empire.

But very little of Carolingian architecture survives—a few small churches in Germany such as Steinbach, Michelstadt and Höchst, then Germigny-des-Prés in France, which is, with its horseshoe apses, a curious Spanish exclave on French soil, and finally that part of the cathedral of Aachen (Aix-la-Chapelle) which was the chapel of one of Charlemagne's palaces originally connected with the Great Hall (not now traceable beyond parts of the foundation walls) by colonnades nearly 400 ft. long (pl. II B). An equestrian statue of Theodoric looted from Rome was significantly placed in this colonnaded forecourt, and columns of the chapel also came from Italy. So did undoubtedly its ground plan. There can be little doubt that the architect took his inspiration from S. Vitale. But he could see no sense in the curved-out niches, so he flattened them out, thus re-establishing the straightforward division between central octagon and ambulatory. He also eliminated the columns on the ground floor. Simple wide openings alternate with short, sturdy piers. The plainness and massiveness of this ground floor (and also of the giant niche of the façade) strike a note utterly different from the subtle spatial harmonies of S. Vitale. Yet the upper floors with their polished antique columns, superimposed in two orders, re-echo something of the transparency, and the floating of space from one unit into another, which make the beauty of Justinian's churches.

Aachen was consecrated in 805, the large Abbey church of Centula (or St. Riquier) near Abbeville in 799. It seems, according to an old engraving and still older description—for the building itself no longer stands—to have possessed features more original and more vigorously progressive than the Palatine chapel. It was certainly not modelled on the Early Christian pattern. Neither its double crossings with their double towers, nor its double transepts, one near the East, one near the West end, have Italian or Oriental antecedents. However, our knowledge of Centula is too dim to efface the evidence of Aachen, the other church plan, and Charlemagne's palace plans. All we can say is that a new primitive Western plainness and massiveness loomed behind the polished façade of a Roman revival.

Charlemagne's architecture taken as a whole can no more than his Empire be accepted as the real start of the Middle Ages. It appears a premature flowering doomed to wither under the grim frosts of the later 9th and the 10th centuries. Less than thirty years after Charlemagne's death in 814 the

Empire was divided. France and Germany henceforth took separate courses. But internal struggles, earl against earl, duke against duke, shook both. And from outside, the Vikings ravaged the North-West—Normans they called them in France, Danes in England—the Hungarians menaced the East, the Saracens, i.e., Mohammedan Arabs, the South. No progress was possible in art and architecture. What we know is almost as primitive as Merovingian work, although forms taken up under Charlemagne and his immediate successors were still used. But the spirit in which they were used was blunt and crude. And since during the pre-Carolingian centuries intercourse with Roman architecture had not entirely ceased, the period between about 850 and 950 seems even more barbaric.

Not much of this dark age has stood the ravages of war and the zeal of later builders in France and Germany. To see greater numbers of 9th- and 10th-century buildings in anything like their original state one must go to the borderlands of Western civilisation, to Spain and Britain.

In Spain the Visigoths, rulers from the 5th to the early 8th century, had built churches of an oddly mutilated basilican type. S. Juan de Baños, for example, dedicated in 661, consisted originally (fig. 3 shows the plan before the later alterations) of a short nave separated from the aisles by arcades with horseshoe arches, exaggeratedly projecting transepts, a square apse, two rectangular Eastern chapels or vestries inorganically detached from the apse, and as another inorganic appendix a rectangular West porch. There is no spatial flow nor even a unity of plan in this minute building. The exterior colonnades originally running along the North, South and West walls are of Late Antique-Oriental origin, as incidentally is the horseshoe arch.

This motive however the Arabs, when they conquered the South of Spain in the 8th century, made so much their own that for several centuries to come it remained the hallmark of Mohammedan and Mozarabic, i.e., Christian Spanish, architecture under Arab influence. The Arabs, as against the Vikings and Hungarians, were far from uncivilised. On the contrary, their religion, their science, and their cities, especially Cordova with her half-million inhabitants, were far ahead of those of 8th-century Franks in France or Asturians in Northern Spain. The Mosque at Cordova (786–990), a building of eleven aisles, each twelve bays long, with interlaced arches and complicated star-ribbed vaults, has a filigree elegance more in keeping with the spatial

Fig. 3.—S. Juan de Baños, dedicated 661. The east parts have later been altered. Overall length 63 ft.

transparency of S. Vitale than of the sturdy uncouthness of the North.

Thus while both British and Spanish architecture from the 9th to the early 11th century are provincial compared with the buildings of France and the Rhineland, the Asturias have, owing to their proximity to Mohammedan sophistication, a certain airiness here and there which is absent in Britain. At S. Maria de Naranco near Leon, for example (pl. III and IV A) the fluted buttresses outside—as a structural device and a decorative motif still remotely evocative of Rome—and the slender arcade inside which now separates nave from choir are in a strange contrast to the heavy barrel-vault, the odd shield-like or seal-like medallions from which spring the transverse arches of the vault and the clumsy spiral shafts with their crude block capitals along the walls.

The building incidentally is of very special interest, in so far as in all probability it was designed between 842 and 848 as a Royal Hall for Ramiro I of Asturias—the only surviving early mediaeval example of such a building. It has a low vaulted cellar or crypt, and above this the hall proper, now the nave of the church. This is reached by flights of outside steps leading to porches in the centres of both the long sides of the building. On the East and the West there were originally open loggias, communicating with the main room by arcades, of which one, as has been said before, survives. The present choir is in fact one of the loggias blocked up towards the outside.

In British 9th- and 10th-century architecture one would look in vain for such subtleties. Where buildings are preserved complete or nearly complete, we can see that their ground plans were just as elementary. At Bradford-on-Avon (fig. 4) e.g., the nave has no aisles. The chancel is accessible from the nave only by a narrow door with crudely-worked joints. The porches on the North and South sides are also separated from the main room. Compartment is added to compartment, very much as in the Visigothic churches of Spain. Anglo-Saxon decoration is just as elementary. The craftsmen who worked the Ruthwell Cross in Bede's time seem superior to those who, one or two generations before the Conquest, decorated the tower of Earl's Barton. The only structural part of its decoration is the emphasizing of the three stories by plain string courses (pl. IV B). All the rest, the wooden-looking strips arranged in rows vertically like beanstalks, or higher up in crude lozenge patterns, is structurally senseless. Yet they are in a similar relation to Carolingian architecture as Asturian decoration was to the Muslim style. But while the day-to-day proximity of Arab to Spanish civilisation created the mixed idiom of Naranco and the Mozarabic style of the 10th century, the British builders reduced the Romanising motifs of Carolingian decoration to ungainly

Fig. 4.—Bradford-on-Avon, an Anglo-Saxon church plan.
Length inside 42 ft.

rusticity.   The so-called long-and-short work up the edges of Earl's Barton tower and so many other contemporary English towers is another indication of the rawness of the minds and the heaviness of the hands of these late Anglo-Saxon architects, if architects they can be called.

CHAPTER TWO

THE ROMANESQUE STYLE
(c. 1000–1200)

Yet during these dark and troubled years the foundations of mediæval civilisation were laid. The feudal system grew, one does not know from what roots, until it had become the framework round which all social life of the Middle Ages was built, a system as characteristic and unique as mediæval religion and mediæval art, strictly binding lord and vassal, and yet so vague, so dependent on symbolical gestures that we to-day can hardly recognise it as a system at all. By the end of the 10th century it had received its final form. By then political stability too had been re-established in the Empire. Otto the Great was crowned in Rome in 962. At the same time the first of the reform movements of monasticism set out from Cluny in Burgundy. And again at the same time the Romanesque style was created.

To describe an architectural style it is necessary to describe its individual features. But the features alone do not make the style. There must be one central idea active in all of them. Thus several of the most significant Early Roman-

Fig. 5.—Tours: S. Martin's. The thick black lines are the walls of the church begun shortly after 997, dedications in 1014 and 1020. The chancel with ambulatory and apses was c. 55 ft. wide (approximate overall width of choir and ambulatory 70 feet).

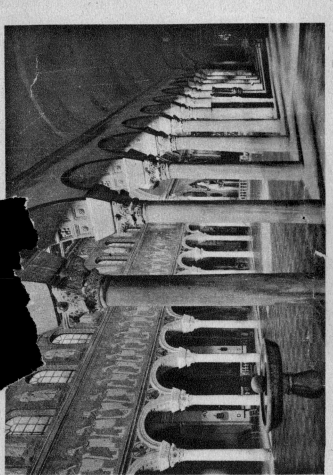

Ravenna, S. Apollinare Nuovo, early 6th century.

A. Ravenna, S. Vitale, compl[...] [...]el of Charlemagne's palace), consecrated 805.

Santa Maria de Naranco, built as a Royal Hall some time before 848.

Winchester Cathedral, north transept, 1079–93

Durham Cathedral, nave, early 12th century

A. Worms Cathedral on the Rhine, *c.* 1175–1250. *B.* Cluny, Abbey Church, in Burgundy. The east end as, according to the excavations and research of the Mediæval Academy of America, it was at the beginning of the 12th century. (Illustrated from Professor K. Conant's drawing by courtesy of Professor Conant.)

Vézelay, Burgundy, La Madeleine, early 12th century.

separated from the nave by arcades that have an alternation of supports, pillars to stress the corners of the squares, columns in between. Each transept again consisted of a centre square flanked by a rectangle. The centre squares were clearly singled out by means of chancel arches not only to the East and West, but also to the North and South. In later buildings each transept was to be square too, and the aisles consisted of sequences of squares. On the east side at Hildesheim a square chancel was inserted between crossing and apse. Chapels branched off the transepts parallel to the main apses—a complex ground plan, yet fully ordered by an active conquering power of reason.

Who conceived this "metrical system" we do not know. What we do know, however, and have no reason to question, is the fact, recorded by his biographer, that St. Bernward, the bishop who was responsible for the building of St. Michael's, was " foremost in writing, experienced in painting, excellent in the science and art of bronze founding and in all architectural work ". Similarly we know, e.g., of Aethelwold, the great English bishop, that he was a " theoreticus architectus ", well versed in the building and repairing of monasteries, of Benno, Bishop of Osnabruck in the 11th century, that he was " an outstanding architect, a skilful planner (' dispositor ') of masonry work ". We also still possess the ground plan which, about the year 835, had been sent by some bishop or abbot close to the Emperor's court to the abbot of St. Gall in Switzerland as an ideal scheme (" exemplar ") for the re-building of his monastery. Such and many similar contemporary references justify the view that, while actual building operations were of course at all times the job of the craftsman, the designing of churches and monasteries in the early Middle Ages may often have been due to clerics—at least to the same extent to which Lord Burlington was responsible for the design of his villa in Chiswick. After all, during those centuries nearly all the literati, the educated, the sensitive were clerics.

The same tendency towards an elementary articulation which the new ground plans reveal can be found in the elevations of the 11th-century churches. At St. Michael's, Hildesheim, the system of alternating supports, the rhythm

of *a b b a b b a* (*a* representing square piers and *b* columns)
serves to divide up the long stretch of wall, and ultimately
the space enclosed by the walls, into separate units. This
system became the customary one in Central European
Romanesque architecture. In the West, and especially
in England, another equally effective method was developed
for achieving the same aim. It had been created in Normandy early in the 11th century. The Normans by then
had lived in the North-West of France for a hundred years
and from being Viking adventurers had become rulers of
a large territory, clear-minded, determined and progressive,
adopting French achievements where they saw possibilities
in them—this applies to the French language, suppler than
their own, to feudalism and to the reform of Cluny—and
imbuing them with the energy of their native spirit. They
conquered Sicily and parts of Southern Italy in the 11th and
12th centuries and created an eminently interesting civiliza-
tion there, a blend of what was most advanced in the
administration of Normandy and in the thought and habits
of the Saracens. In the meantime they had also conquered
England, to replace there by their own superior mode of life
that of the Northern invaders who had come before them.
The Norman style in architecture, the most consistent
variety of the Romanesque style in the West, strongly
influenced France during the 11th century; in England it
did more than that: it made English mediæval architecture.
One cannot discuss the Romanesque style without taking
into consideration English Norman cathedrals and abbey
churches. French writers too often forget that. The
fulfilment of what had been initiated at Jumièges about
1030 and Caen about 1050 lies at Ely, at Winchester, at
Durham, to mention only a few.

The new principle was the separation of bay from bay by
tall shafts running through from the floor to the ceiling—a
flat ceiling almost everywhere; for the art of vaulting the
width of a nave was all but lost. Thus again an articulation
was achieved that conveys to us at once a feeling of certainty
and stability. There is no wavering here—as there was none
in the ruthless policy of William the Conqueror in subduing
and normanizing England. Blunt, massive and over-

whelmingly strong are the individual forms which architects used in these early buildings, sacred as well as secular. For the Norman keep, the other architectural type which the Normans brought from France, has got the same compactness, the same disdain of embellishment as the Norman church. There were of course reasons of defence for the bareness of the keep, but it was a matter of expression, i.e., of æsthetics, too, as a comparison with such a piece of building as the transept of Winchester Cathedral (*c.* 1080–90) proves. At Winchester (pl. v) the solid wall, though opened up in arcades on the ground floor and the gallery floor and again in a passage-way in front of the clerestory window, remains the primary fact. We feel its

Fig. 8.—Winchester Cathedral: Capital, *c.* 1080–1090.

mighty presence everywhere. The talls shafts are bound to it and are themselves massive like enormous tree trunks. The columns of the gallery openings are short and sturdy, their capitals rude blocks (fig. 8), the simplest statement of the fact that here something of round section was to be linked up with something of square section. This plainness is typical of the 11th century, a plainness of statement expressed in terms of the plainest of forms.

By the end of the century changes began to appear, all pointing towards a new differentiation. More complex, more varied, more lively forms can be found everywhere. There is perhaps less force in them, but more individual expression. Now comes the age of St. Bernard of Clairvaux (died 1153) who called it his aim as a preacher (and he was one of the greatest of mediæval preachers) to move hearts, not to expound scripture, the age of Abelard (died

1142), the first to write an autobiographical account of his personal problems of love and scholarship, and in England the age of Henry II and Thomas Becket (died 1170). They stand before us as human beings; William the Conqueror as a natural phenomenon, irresistible and relentless. Just before 1100—when Western Christianity rallied round the banners of the first Crusade—the pioneer work was done in architecture; Early Romanesque was transformed into High Romanesque. Durham is the crucial monument in England, begun in 1093, the East parts vaulted in 1104, the nave *c.* 1130 (pl. VI). The nave appears higher than it is, because, instead of the flat ceiling usual until then and usual in England for some time to come, it is covered by a rib-vault. As our eyes follow the lines of the shafts upwards, this movement does not come to a standstill where the walls end, but is carried further up with the ribs. The vaults of Durham choir are the earliest rib-vaults of Europe. In this lies Durham's eminence in the history of building construction.

Engineering skill had developed considerably during the century between the earliest examples of the Romanesque style and 1100. To vault in stone naves of basilican churches was the ambition of the craftsmen, for reasons of safety against fires in church roofs as well as for reasons of appearance. The Romans had known how to vault on a large scale; but in the West there were before the late 11th century only vaulted apses, small and narrow barrel-vaulted naves (e.g. Naranco, see p. 27), and barrel- or cross-vaulted aisles. Now the vaulting of the wider naves of major churches was mastered, and—as always happens when an innovation is the full expression of the spirit of an age—mastered independently by several ingenious architects in several centres of building activity at about the same time. Burgundy remained faithful to massive barrel vaults. The earliest that can be dated seem to belong to about 1065; those at Cluny, when this mightiest monastery of Europe was rebuilt, about 1100, had the widest span anywhere. Speyer, the imperial cathedral on the Rhine, received her first cross-vaults in the eighties. And then there is Durham. A good deal of controversy still remains about dates of early vaults; the new powerful initiative of the late 11th century however is beyond doubt.

Now the most remarkable fact about the vaults of Durham is that rib-vaults as against ribless cross-vaults are accepted as one of the *leitmotivs* of the Gothic style. Their structural advantages, just like those of pointed arches and buttresses, lie in the fact that they concentrate thrusts along specially chosen lines and leave the masonry between stretched out like the canvas of a tent from post to post. Thus great saving in stone could be achieved. Hence the Gothic style appears to most people as a constructional affair exclusively. Durham proves this materialistic theory to be wrong. The ribs here are not built up independently, the filling masonry is not lighter. The motif is there, but its constructional application has not yet been discovered. The reason of the Durham builders for introducing so telling a feature must have been the very fact that it is so telling, that it represents the ultimate fulfilment of that tendency towards articulation which had driven Romanesque architects forward for over a hundred years. Now the bay has become a unity not only by the two-dimensional means of lines of demarcation along the walls, but by the three-dimensional means of those diagonal arches set across. Where the two arches meet, where later architects inserted their bosses, there each unified bay has its centre. We move along through the cathedral, not driven towards the altar without halt as in Early Christian churches but stepping from spatial compartment to spatial compartment in a new measured rhythm.

The rib-vault imparts indeed to the whole structure a liveliness opposed to the weight of inert wall so oppressive in 11th-century interiors. This liveliness is taken up in the more animated expression of the arcades and their mouldings, and the introduction of a few sharp ornamental forms, the zig-zag above all. Still, in spite of this quickening of rhythm Durham is far from playful or busy. The circular pillars of the arcades are still of overpowering strength, their sheer bulk being emphasised by the elementary decoration, lozenges, zig-zags, flutes exquisitely carved into their surfaces. The fact, incidentally, that all ornament at

Durham is abstract, is typical only of Norman architecture in England and Normandy, not of Romanesque architecture in general. In France many types of foliated decoration, especially of capitals, exist. The best-known instance in England is characteristically enough in the crypt of Canterbury, the gateway through which a Continental style had passed once before about 600, and another one was going to pass in 1175. The capitals here (fig. 9) have foliated decoration, and some even beasts. But nature had no immediate influence on these. They derive from sample-books kept in the lodges of the masons and based on illuminated manuscripts, ivories, previous work of the lodge, etc. Originality was a conception unknown, so was observation of nature. Style as a restrictive force of discipline

Fig. 9.—Canterbury Cathedral: Capital, 12th century.

ruled as unchallenged as authority in religion. Still, Durham seems more humane than Winchester, and 12th-century capitals more humane than the block-shapes of the 11th, just as the sermons of St. Bernard seem more humane and more personal than those of the theologians before him.

The exterior of Durham Cathedral is one of the most magnificent sights of England. There it stands, flanked on one side by the Bishop's Castle, on the top of its steep wooded hill with its mighty tower over the crossing and the two slenderer Western towers to balance its weight. They are not Norman in their present form, the Western towers dating from the 13th, the central tower (originally with a spire) from the 15th century. But towers were planned from the beginning, and where they were carried out, they ended in spires of moderate pitch such as those at Southwell (cf. pl. VII B). The outside appearance of Romanesque churches thus differed just as widely from that of Early Christian churches as their interiors. While at S. Apollinare Nuovo the exterior hardly mattered—even church towers, when they were introduced, stood separate from their churches—a few Carolingian and then most larger Romanesque churches were designed to display variety and magnificence outside as well as inside. St. Michael's at Hildesheim with its two choirs, towers over both crossings and staircase turrets on both ends of both transepts, is the earliest surviving example of a truly Romanesque exterior. Later German cathedral architects took great pride in the vigour of exterior grouping (pl. VII A), usually on the Hildesheim principle of accents over and near the crossings.

The other main accent was the façade. Here early in the 11th century the two-tower pattern was conceived. Strasbourg seems to have had it in 1015; at St. Stephen's, Caen, a splendid example of about 1065–1080 survives. Such fronts are meant to arrest us, not simply to draw us inside as did the Early Christian front which was hardly more than a walled-up cross-section through the interior. East ends were sometimes equally varied and arresting. On the grandest scale must have been the scheme at Cluny, where the church was rebuilt at the end of the 11th century (pl. VII B). There were two transepts (as later became the rule in English cathedrals), each with an octagonal tower over the crossing. The more important of these, the one further West, had octagonal towers to the right and left of the crossing as well (one of these survives), and two Eastern apses to each arm. The Eastern transept had four apses too. Moreover, the chancel apse had an ambulatory with five radiating chapels. Thus one saw looking at the church from the East a graded development in many carefully proportioned steps from the low radiating chapels over the ambulatory, the main apse, the chancel roof, the tower over the eastern crossing, to the tallest tower further West—a structure so complex, so polyphonous, as earlier centuries in the West could not have conceived, and the Greeks would have detested. Yet as it was before its destruction in 1810, and now stands before our minds' eyes in Professor K. J.

Conant's, the American archeologist's, reconstruction,* Cluny must have been the ideal expression of that proudest moment of mediæval Christianity, when the reform had conquered the throne of the popes, and Cluniac popes had humiliated the emperors and called up the knights of Europe to defend the Holy Land in the first Crusade (1095).

As varied and lively as the appearance of the individual church in the 12th century was the development of the Romanesque style in the different territories of the West. In England, the Norman system was universally accepted, tenser and more erect than any other; Germany built cross-vaulted basilicas on the metrical system of Hildesheim. As for what is now France, about half-a-dozen local schools can be distinguished. This is not surprising, as a unified France came into being only in the course of the 13th century. The most important schools are those of Provence, Aquitaine (i.e., the South-West), Auvergne, Burgundy and Normandy. Their comparatively static customs were crossed by a strong current from the North and West of France right down to the far North-West of Spain, the current of the principal pilgrimage routes. Pilgrimages were one of the chief media of cultural communication in the Middle Ages, and their effects on church planning are evident. They can be seen from Chartres via Orléans, Tours, Poitiers, Saintes to Spain; from Vézelay via Le Puy, Conques, or via Périgueux to Moissac and on to Spain; and from Arles to St. Gilles and Toulouse and then to Spain. The goal was Santiago de Compostela, a sanctuary as celebrated as Jerusalem and Rome. The Cluniac order had much to do with the development of the pilgrimage routes, and characteristics of Cluny can be found in the chief monasteries all the way along. The plan of Tours, with ambulatory and radiating chapels, is one of the recurring motifs in the pilgrimage sanctuaries—regardless of whether it blended with local customs.

In the South and South-West, for example, no such compromise could be arrived at; for the school of Provence

* The reconstruction which Professor Conant very kindly allowed me to illustrate here is based on the excavations conducted by him for the Mediæval Academy of America.

liked barrel-vaulted churches without any aisles, or occasionally with aisles the same height as the nave, and Aquitaine
went in for naves consisting of several domed bays, also as a
rule without aisles or with aisles of nave height. In
Auvergne aisles are also as a rule as high as the nave, but
they do not look it, because they have galleries. Burgundy
(in accordance with her geographical position between
Provence, the North Italian sphere of influence, and the
Rhineland) kept to the Basilican tradition and used for
vaulting either barrel vaults or cross vaults. Cluny
belonged to the first kind; Vézelay, begun in 1096 and completed, it seems, in 1132, is one of the grandest examples
of the second (pl. VIII). The church was supposed to
possess the relics of the Magdalen; they made it a favourite
goal of pilgrimages. It lies majestically on a hill over-
shadowing the houses of the minute town. The main
entrance is through an aisled narthex or galilee of three
bays and on through one of the wildest of Romanesque
figure portals. The nave has nothing of that violence.
With its later and lighter choir in the far distance, its length
of about 200 ft. between narthex and crossing, its unusually
high nave vaults, its arches of alternating grey and white
courses, and its inexhaustible profusion of capitals with
sacred stories, it possesses a quick and lively rhythm and
a proud magnificence without being less robust than
Durham.

Centrally planned churches are a great exception during
the Middle Ages. The most outstanding of them in France
is St. Front at Périgueux (pl. IX A). Here, probably during
the second quarter of the 12th century, the classic expression
of Romanesque clarity and determination was achieved.*
The ground plan is a Greek cross, a square for the centre,
four squares for the arms. Each square has in its turn again
short arms and is covered by a vast dome. There is no
sculptural decoration except for some arcading along the

---

* The term *classic* is used throughout in this book with a meaning
different from *classical*. *Classical* applies to anything inspired by, or
copied from, the style of Antiquity, *classic* to the short moments of
perfect balance achieved by many styles. When we say of a work of
literature or art that it is *a classic*, we mean something similar, namely
that it is perfect of its kind, and universally accepted as such.

walls. The system, in its purity unique in France, is copied from S. Marco in Venice begun in 1063. There, however, where it stands in the centre of the most oriental and most romantic of European cities, as an outpost of Byzantine architecture, it has all the magic of the East, mosaics, luxuriant capitals, arcades to separate centres from arms, and concealed spatial relations in the sense which we have seen at Ravenna. At Périgueux it is stripped of all that suspicious glamour and appears pure and sheer, great for its architectural nobility and none other. There is something strikingly Roman in this bareness. No wonder that the ground plan was re-invented in almost identical form by the Italians of the Renaissance.

Of the Romanesque style of Italy the most important varieties are the Lombard and the Tuscan. The Lombard is the powerful expression of the spirit of one of Europe's most prosperous regions. Its influence extended deep into Spain and Germany. Its strongest expression is S. Ambrogio in Milan, with a low squat nave and massive piers. Its wide domed cross-vaults have broad primitive ribs. Should they really be in their present form of the late 11th century, they would be a remarkable historical parallel to Durham. There are plenty of other cathedrals in the towns on or near the Po. Their interior characteristics are cross vaults, galleries in the aisles, polygonal domes over the crossings, their outside characteristics isolated towers (*campanile* is their Italian name), and miniature arcadings, especially round the apses just below the eaves and along the façades just below the gables. The extreme case of such decorative arcading is the front and the leaning tower of the cathedral of Pisa in Tuscany.

This is however a monument of a rather alien character—Oriental more than Tuscan. To appreciate the truly Tuscan spirit in its Romanesque manifestation one has to look at such buildings as S. Miniato al Monte in Florence (pl. xxi), which, in spite of its early date (it may even be contemporary with the transept of Winchester, pl. v), possesses a delicacy of treatment, a civilised restraint in sculptural decoration and a susceptibility to the spirit of Antiquity unparalleled anywhere in the North—a first synthesis of Tuscan intellect and grace with Roman simplicity and poise.

Yet in those parts of France in which classical remains abound and men, climate and scenery strike one as so akin to Italy, a new sympathy with the heritage of Rome also appeared with the end of the 11th century. The most important monuments of this blend of the Romanesque and the Roman stand in Burgundy and Provence. The capitals of the Burgundian church of St. Lazare at Autun (fig. 10) show a live understanding of the vegetal and decorative character of the acanthus leaf which, but for a few rare Early Carolingian exceptions, had not been achieved by

Fig. 10.—Autun: St. Lazare: Capital, late 11th century.

the West since the decline of the Roman Empire. A similar understanding, not of Roman detail, but of Roman architecture as a whole distinguishes the façade of St. Gilles in Provence (pl. IX B). For while its three round-headed porches and the manifold mouldings to their arches are unmistakably Romanesque, the columns in front of the walls between the doorways have straight entablatures, a feature of antique, never of Western architecture, and luxuriant Corinthian capitals. Moreover, there are figures of saints standing upright in straight-headed recesses. Life-size sculpture had been the greatest achievement of Classical Antiquity. In the days of S. Apollinare Nuovo it had all but disappeared. There is no large-scale Carolingian figure sculpture either.   Only during the 11th century, when the plastic sense returned to church architecture, it re-appeared, only towards its end it began to produce work of an æsthetic standard equalling that of the buildings themselves, and only centuries later did it gain independence from architecture.

CHAPTER THREE

THE EARLY AND CLASSIC GOTHIC STYLE
(*c.* 1150–*c.* 1250)

In 1140 the foundation stone was laid for the new choir of St. Denis Abbey near Paris (fig. 11). It was consecrated in 1144. Abbot Suger, the mighty counsellor of two Kings of France, was the soul of the enterprise. There are few buildings in Europe so revolutionary in their conception and so rapid and unhesitating in their execution. Four years was an exceptionally short time in the 12th century for rebuilding the choir of a large abbey church. Whoever designed the choir of St. Denis, one can safely say, invented the Gothic style, although Gothic features had existed before, scattered here and there, and, in the centre of France, the provinces around St. Denis, even developed with a certain consistency.

The features which make up the Gothic style are well enough known, too well in fact, because most people forget that a style is not an aggregate of features, but an integral

Fig. 11.—St. Denis: Abbey Church, consecrated 1144. Overall width *c.* 95 ft.

whole.   Still, it may be just as well to recapitulate them and
re-examine their meaning.   They are the pointed arch, the
buttress, the flying buttress, and the rib-vault.   The pointed
arch makes it possible to vault bays of other than square
plan without getting into trouble about the level heights for
the arches.   With rounded arches the mason who is dealing
with a narrow rectangular bay has to stilt some of his arches
or depress some to achieve level heights.   Now all this could
be adjusted by varying the degree of pointing.   Ribs made
it possible to reduce a stone vault to a few supporting lines
holding each other in position, with light, thin panels of
masonry between them.   Buttresses served to take over the
weight of the vault as concentrated in the ribs, and lead it
downwards, thus achieving the same for the walls as the ribs
do for the roof, i.e., reducing them to non-supporting panels
which could be built lightly or indeed be replaced by glass.
Flying buttresses were invented to transfer the vertical
thrust from the vault on to the more distant buttresses of the
aisles instead of leaving it to press downwards vertically on
the clerestory walls and the arcades of the nave beneath.
The piers of the arcades could, thanks to the flying buttresses,
be made much taller and slenderer than ever before.

The whole was a most logical and ingenious system, more
scientific and more abstract than any constructional device
of antiquity.   Yet it was not created by the engineer, as it
were, for technical reasons.   It is wrong to say that the
Gothic style is the outcome of such material innovations.
On the contrary, it has been pointed out that the material
innovations came later than the spiritual desire for a new
kind of expression.   Architects wished to enliven inert
masses of masonry and to quicken spatial motion.   For
these and no other reasons they introduced shafts to articulate walls and ribs to articulate vaults.

It is only at St. Denis that Gothic construction and Gothic
motifs are linked up with each other to form a Gothic
system.   The consequence is at once obvious.   Rib-vaults
cover the varying shapes of bays, buttresses replace the
massive walls between the radiating chapels which now
form a continuous wavy fringe to the ambulatory.   Their
side walls have disappeared entirely.   If it were not for the

five-ribbed vaults, one would feel in a second, outer ambulatory, with exceedingly shallow chapels. The effect inside the church is one of lightness, of air circulating freely, of supple curves and energetic concentration. No longer is part demonstratively separated from part. Articulation remains; nothing is vague; but it is a far more sophisticated articulation. Who was the great genius to conceive this? Was it Abbot Suger himself who so proudly wrote a little book about the building and consecration of his church? Hardly; for the Gothic as against the Romanesque style is so essentially based on a co-operation between artist and engineer, and a synthesis of æsthetic and technical qualities, that only a man of profound structural knowledge can have invented such a system. We are here at the beginning of a specialisation that has gone on splitting up our activities into smaller and smaller competencies, until to-day the patron is not an architect, the architect not a builder, the builder not a mason, let alone such distinctions as those between the heating engineer, the air-conditioning engineer, the electrical installation expert and the sanitation expert.

The new type of architect to whom St. Denis and the later French and English cathedrals must be ascribed is the master craftsman as a recognised artist. Creative master craftsmen had of course existed before, and probably always designed most of what was built. But their status now began to change. It was a very gradual development. Suger in his book does not say one word about the architect of St. Denis, nor in fact about the designer of the Church as such. It seems curious; surely he must have known very well what a daring work he had put up. To explain his silence one must remember the often-quoted and often-misunderstood anonymity of the Middle Ages. It does not mean of course that cathedrals grew like trees. They were all designed by someone. But in the earlier mediæval centuries the names of these men, immortal as their work seemed, did not count. They were content to be workmen working for a cause greater than their own fame. However, during the 12th and above all the 13th centuries the self-confidence of the individual grew, and personality came to be appreciated. The names of the architects of

Rheims and Amiens Cathedrals were recorded in a curious way on the pavement of the naves. A preacher complained that master-masons got higher wages than others by simply going about with their staffs in their hands and giving orders, and—he adds—" nihil laborant ", they don't do any work. A century after this the King of France was godfather to the son of one of these men and made a considerable present in gold to him for enabling him to study at a university. But two hundred years had to elapse after the time of Suger to make such intimacy possible.

One of the earliest cases in which we can form a live impression of the personality of one of the great master-masons of the early Gothic style is that of William of Sens, architect to the choir of Canterbury Cathedral—a work as revolutionary in England as St. Denis was in France. A fire had destroyed the old choir in 1174, as we are told by Gervase, the chronicler of the Cathedral, who had himself lived through the events he relates. There was great despair amongst the brethren until after a while they began to consult " by what method the ruined church might be repaired. Architects, both French and English, were assembled ; but they disagreed. Some suggested repair, while others insisted that the whole church must be taken down, if the monks wished to dwell in safety. This overwhelmed them with grief. Among the architects there was one, William of Sens, a man of great abilities and a most ingenious workman in wood and stone. Dismissing the rest, they chose him for the undertaking. And he, residing many days with the monks and carefully surveying the burnt walls . . . did yet for some time conceal what he found necessary to do, lest the truth should kill us in our hopelessness. But he went on preparing all things that were necessary, either himself or by the agency of others. And when he found that the monks began to be somewhat comforted, he confessed that the damaged pillars and all that they supported, must be destroyed, if the monks wished to have a safe and excellent building. At length they agreed . . . to take down the ruined choir. Attention was given to procure stones from abroad. He made the most ingenious machines for loading and unloading ships, and for drawing the mortar and stones.

He delivered also to the masons models (cut-out wooden templates) for cutting the stones. . . ." Then the chronicler tells us exactly what during each of the following four years was done. At the beginning of the fifth year, however, William, while on the scaffolding, fell down to the ground from a height of fifty feet. He was badly hurt and had to " entrust the completion of the work to a certain ingenious monk who was overseer of the rough masons . . .". But though lying in bed, he gave orders " what was

Fig. 12.—From Villard de Honnecourt's textbook, c. 1235.

first and what was last to be done. . . . At length finding no benefit from the skill of his surgeons, he went to France to die at home ", and an English successor was appointed.*

So here we have the craftsman, equally skilled in masonry and engineering work, diplomatic with his patrons and appreciated by them, but never while conducting work abroad forgetting the land of his youth. At Sens, wherefrom he came, a new cathedral had been begun about thirty years before he went over to Canterbury, a cathedral with certain features evidently imitated at Canterbury.

We are fortunate in possessing at least one even more

* The quotations are from Mr. Charles Cotton's edition (Canterbury Papers No. 3. Published by the Friends of Canterbury Cathedral, 1930).

complete record of the personality and work of a Gothic architect, a notebook, or rather textbook, prepared about 1235 by Villard de Honnecourt, an architect from the Cambrai region of Northern France. This textbook, pre-

Fig. 13.—From Villard de Honnecourt's textbook, *c.* 1235.

served at the National Library in Paris, is an eminently personal document. Villard addresses his pupils. He promises them tuition in masonry and carpentry, drawing of architecture and figures, and geometry. Of all this the book contains examples, drawn and briefly described. It is invaluable as a source of information on the methods

and attitude of the 13th century.   Villard, although an
architect, draws a Crucifixion, a Madonna, and figures
of the sleeping disciples as they were represented in the scene
on the Mount of Olives (fig. 13), all these evidently for stone
carvers to work from.   He also drew figures of Pride and
Humility, the Church Triumphant and the Wheel of For-
tune.   But there are worldly scenes too, wrestlers (fig. 12),
men on horseback, a King with his retinue.   Then there are

Fig. 14.—From Villard de Honnecourt's textbook, c. 1235.

many animals, some surprisingly realistic, others quite
fantastic.   There are simple geometrical schemes for
drawing human heads and animals.   He records parts of
buildings, the ground plans of church choirs (fig. 12), a
tower of Laon Cathedral (he says: " I have been in many
countries as you can see from this book, but I have never
seen such another tower "), windows from the choir of
Rheims (fig. 14; he says: " I was on my way to Hungary,
when I drew this, because I liked it best "), and a rose
window at Lausanne.   He traces a labyrinth, and draws

foliage. He designs a foliated end for a choir stall and a lectern with three evangelists. He has diagrams of mouldings and of timber construction. He adds proudly a good many pieces of machinery, a sawmill, a device for lifting heavy weights, and also such automata as a lectern eagle that turns its head, or a heatable metal apple for a bishop to hold in his hand. He even notes a recipe for getting rid of superfluous hair.

Such was the range of knowledge and experience of the men who built the great Gothic cathedrals. They were invited abroad as the bringers of the new Gothic style, the " opus francigenum ", as it is called in a German record of that time; they kept their eyes open while they travelled, and noted buildings, sculptures and paintings with the same eagerness. They knew as much of the carving of figures and ornaments as of building construction, although their drawing technique was still elementary.

St. Denis must owe its novelty and consistency to a master-mason of this calibre. And many a bishop and an architect burned with ambition to emulate Suger and St. Denis. Between 1140 and 1220 new cathedrals were begun on an ever-growing scale at Sens, Noyon, Senlis, and then Paris (Notre Dame, c. 1163 seqq.), Laon (c. 1170 seqq.), Chartres (c. 1195 seqq.), Rheims (1211 seqq.), and Amiens (1220 seqq.). These are by no means all; there are many more. We must, however, here confine ourselves to an analysis of one or two.

The ground plan of Notre Dame in Paris (fig. 15) is characteristically different from that of any Romanesque Cathedral. What is obvious at the first glance, is that the sub-division into a number of clearly separated parts has been given up. Early Romanesque architects introduced this system of elementary articulation to achieve a principle of order out of the floating streams of spatial movement in churches of the centuries before. Now some of this seems to have returned. Bays are again narrow and follow each other in unrelieved uniformity. There are double aisles such as the largest of the Early Christian basilicas had possessed. The transepts keep within the width of these their projection, so characteristic of Romanesque churches is flattened out. The ambulatory is doubled too and had originally no radiating chapels. What we had seen heralded in the shallow sinuosity of the St. Denis chapels is now achieved.

There are, however, two decisive differences between the ground plan of Notre Dame and that of Early Christian churches: the West façade with its two towers, and the transept placed much further West than before, in fact, only just over half-way down the nave. Thus instead of the uninterrupted, magically driven way towards East, a movement results hardly less articulated, though more subtly articulated, than that in a Romanesque cathedral. It is no

Fig. 15.—Paris: Notre Dame, begun *c.* 1163 (top-half ground floor, bottom-half upper floor). Length *c.* 440 ft.

longer split into numerous units which one has to add up mentally, as it were, to summarize the spatial totality, but concentrated in a few, in fact three sections; West, Centre, East. The transept acts as the centre of the balance. The façade and the double ambulatory round the apse are the two scales. But to appreciate the significance of these new features, one must stand in a Gothic cathedral, and then walk round its exterior.

Inside, very few who experience French Gothic of the 13th century for the first time or have not experienced it for some time, will at once feel that balance which the ground plan seemed to reveal. For it is not the happy, seemingly effortless and indestructible balance of the Greeks, but a balance achieved out of two equally vehement drives,

towards two opposed directions. One's first impression at
Amiens (pl. x) built about forty or fifty years after Paris and
marking the summit of the High Gothic style in France, is
one of breath-taking height. In Durham the relation of nave
width to nave height was 1 : 2·3, in Amiens it is 1 : 3·5, the
absolute height in Durham being approximately 80 ft., in
Amiens 140 ft. The drive upward is just as forcible as, or,
owing to the slenderness of all members, even more forcible
than was the drive Eastward in Early Christian churches.
And the Eastward drive has not by any means slackened
either. The narrowness of the arcades and the uniform
shape of the piers do not seem to call for even a momentary
change of direction. They accompany one on one's way,
as closely set and as rapidly appearing and disappearing as
telegraph poles along a railway line. There is not time at
first to stop and admire them. Yet in pressing forward,
the transept halts us and diverts our eyes to the right and
left. Here we stop, here we endeavour for the first time to
take in the whole. In an Early Christian church nothing of
this kind was provided, in a Romanesque church so much
of it that movement went slowly from bay to bay, from compartment to compartment. At Amiens there is only one
such halt, and it cannot be long. Again nave and aisles,
now of the chancel, close round us, and we do not come to
an ultimate rest until we have reached the apse and the
ambulatory, gathering with splendid energy the parallel
streams of East-bound energy and concentrating them in a
final soaring movement along the narrowly spaced piers of
the apse and the narrow East windows up to the giddy
heights of the vault ribs and vaulting bosses.

This description is an attempt at analysing one's spatial
experience in a cathedral such as Amiens or Rheims or
Beauvais, ignoring of course the fact that a normal 13th-
century church-goer would never have been admitted to the
chancel. What will become evident from it, is the tension
of the two dominant directions or dimensions, a tension, to
say it once more, transformed into a precarious balance.
Once one has felt this, one will recognise it in every detail.
The piers are slender and erect, part of the upward drive.
Yet they are round, firm and shapely, with their four

detached shafts and their capitals with exquisite realistic foliage (cf. pl. xv A). The mouldings of the arcades are sharp and manifold with rolls and deep hollows, high lights and black but precise shadows. The clerestory is all opened up into vast sheets of glass. Yet they are subdivided by vigorously moulded shafts and by geometrical tracery. The introduction of tracery, an invention of the Gothic style (cf. fig. 14) is especially telling. For in each window and each group of windows a circle crowns the sharply pointed arches—repose at the end of forceful action. Again in the vaults each boss signifies Gothic balance—the firm knotting of four lines of energy, conducted by shafts and then by ribs.

This balance of high tensions is the classic expression of the Western spirit—as final as the temple of the 5th century B.C. was that of the Greek spirit. Then it was rest and blissful harmony, now it is activity, only just for one moment held in suspense. And it requires concentrated effort to master the contrasts and partake of the balance. Like a Bach fugue, a Gothic cathedral demands all our emotional and intellectual powers. Now we find ourselves lost in the mystical ruby and emerald glow of translucent stained glass, and now called back to alert attention by the precise course of thin yet adequately strong lines. What is the secret of these vast temples? Is it in their miraculous interiors with vast stone vaults at an immense height, walls all of glass, and arcades much too slim and tall to carry them? The Greek architect achieved a harmony of load and support convincing at once and for ever, the Gothic architect, far bolder constructionally, with his Western soul of the eternal explorer and inventor, always lured by the untried, aims at a contrast between an interior all spirit and an exterior all intellect. For inside the cathedral we cannot and are not meant to understand the law governing the whole. Outside we are faced with a frank exposition of the complicated structural mechanism. The flying buttresses and buttresses, though by no means without the fascination of intricate pattern, will chiefly appeal to reason, conveying a sensation similar to that of the theatre-goer looking at the stage apparatus behind the scenes.

One need hardly point out in so many words how exactly the Gothic cathedral re-echoes in all this the achievements of Western thought in the 13th century, the achievements, i.e., of classic Scholasticism.   Scholasticism is the name for the characteristically mediæval blend of divinity and philosophy. It grew up with the Romanesque style, the centuries before the 11th having in the main not done more than simplify, regroup, and here and there modify the doctrines of the Fathers of the Church and the philosophers and poets of Rome.   During the 12th century, when the Gothic style was created and spread, Scholasticism developed into something just as lofty and at the same time just as intricate as the new cathedrals.   The first half of the 13th century saw the appearance of the compendia of all worldly and sacred knowledge, St. Thomas Aquinas's *Summa*, and the works of Albert the Great and St. Bonaventura, the *Specula* of Vincent of Beauvais, and in poetry Wolfram's *Parsival*.

One of these encyclopædic tomes, the *De Proprietatibus Rerum* by the English Dominican Bartholomæus Anglicus, written about 1240, begins with a chapter on the essence, unity and the three persons of God.   The next chapter deals with the angels, the third with Man, his soul and senses. There follow chapters on the elements and temperaments, on anatomy and physiology, on the Ages of Man, on food, sleep, and similar physical needs, on diseases, on Sun, Moon, Stars and Zodiac, on Time and its divisions, on matter, fire, air, water, on the birds of the air, the fishes of the water, the beasts of the land, on geography, on minerals, trees, colours, tools.   Vincent of Beauvais, who writes about 1250, divides his work into the Mirrors of Nature, of Doctrine, and of History.   And just as the Mirror of Nature starts from God and Creation, so the Mirror of History starts from the Fall of Man, and leads up to the Last Judgment.   The cathedral was—besides being a strictly architectural monument of the spirit of its age— another *Summa*, another *Speculum*, an encyclopædia carved in stone.   The Virgin stood at the centre post of the centre portal of Rheims Cathedral (pl. XII).   Figures were placed into the jambs of this portal representing the Annunciation, the Visitation, the Presentation in the Temple.   High up in the gables of the three portals appear the Crucifixion, the Coronation of the Virgin, and the Last Judgment. But there are also in the Gothic cathedrals, the lives of Christ, the Virgin and Saints told in the stained glass of the windows, and, spread over the plinths, the jambs, the voussoirs, and up against the buttresses, Saints with their attributes by which they are recognised—St. Peter with the key, St. Nicholas with the three golden balls, St. Barbara with the tower, St. Margaret with the Dragon—and scenes and figures from the Old Testament, the Creation of Man, Jonah with the Whale, or Abraham and Melchisedek, and the Roman Sybils who had foretold, it was believed, the coming of Christ, and the Wise and the Foolish Virgins, and the Seven Liberal Arts, and the Months of the Year with their occupations—the grafting of trees, sheep-shearing, harvesting, pig-slaughtering—and the signs of the Zodiac, and the Elements. The Profane and the Sacred—a compendium of knowledge; but everything, as St. Thomas puts it, " ordered towards God ". For Jonah is represented, not because he comes into the Old Testament, but because his three days inside the Whale represent the resurrection of Christ, as Melchisedek offering bread and wine to Abraham represented the Last Supper. To the mediæval mind everything was a symbol. The meaning that mattered lay behind the outward appearance. The simile of the two swords, the Emperor's and the Pope's, was a symbolic expression of political theories. To Gulielmus Durandus the cruciform church represented the Cross, and the weather-cock on the spire the preacher who rouses the sleeping from the night of sin. The mortar, he says, consists of lime, that is love, sand that is earthly toil which love has taken upon itself, and water uniting heavenly love and our earthly world.

All this one must keep in mind to realize how alien this world is to ours, despite all enthusiasm for the cathedrals and their sculptures. We are liable to a reaction in these vast halls which is far too romantic, nebulous, sentimental, whereas to the cleric of the 13th century everything was probably lucid. Lucid, but transcendental. That is the antagonism which defeats us in our age of agnosticism. In the 13th century the bishop and the monk, the knight and the craftsman believed firmly—though each to the measure of his capacity—that nothing exists in the world which does not come from God, and derive its sense and sole interest from its divine meaning.   The mediæval conception of truth was fundamentally different from ours.   Truth was not what can be proved, but what conformed to an accepted revelation.   Research was not conducted to find truth, but to penetrate more deeply into a pre-established truth.   Hence authorities meant more to the mediæval scholar than to anyone now, and hence also the faith of the mediæval artist in the " *exemplar* ", the example to be copied.   Neither originality nor the study of Nature counted for much. Even Villard de Honnecourt copied in nine out of ten of his pages.   Innovations came by degrees and much less deliberately than we can imagine.

Yet the Gothic style surely was a deliberate innovation and the work of strong and self-confident personalities. Its forms allow us to assume that, and we find in fact within scholasticism as the chief innovation of the 13th century, a marked departure from the purely transcendental attitude of the Romanesque and earlier centuries. St. Peter Damiani, in the first half of the 11th century, had said: " The world is so filthy with vices that any holy mind is befouled by even thinking of it ".   Now Vincent of Beauvais exclaims : " How great is even the humblest beauty of this world!   I am moved with spiritual sweetness towards the Creator and Ruler of this world, when I behold the magnitude and beauty and permanence of his creation ".   And beauty according to St. Thomas Aquinas (or a close follower of his philosophy) " consists of a certain consonance of diverging elements ".

But it is never—not yet—the beauty of the world as such that is praised.   It is the beauty of God's creation.   We can enjoy it whole-heartedly, for God himself " rejoices in all things, because everyone is in actual agreement with His Being " (St. Thomas).   Thus stone-carvers could now portray the loveliest leaves, the thorn, the oak, the maple, the vine (pl. xv A).   When St. Peter Damiani wrote, ornament was abstract or severely stylised.   Now youthful life pulses in it, as it pulses in shafts and ribs. But the ornament of the 13th century is even at its most naturalistic, neither petty, nor pedantic. It is still subordinate, never forward, always ministering to a greater cause, that of religious architecture.

Yet it would not have been possible at an earlier age than that of St. Francis's song to Brother Sun and Sister Earth and Brother Wind, than that of the " *Dolce stil nuovo* ", and the French epics of chivalry. The earliest monastic orders had lived in the seclusion of their cloisters, the new orders of the 13th century, the Dominicans and Franciscans, had their monasteries in towns and preached to the burghers. The first Crusades had been called up to liberate the Holy Land, the fourth, the one of 1203, was deflected by the Venetians to Constantinople, which they needed for the benefit of their commerce. But still in the fifth there was in the person of the French King Louis IX, St. Louis, a true Christian Knight, a hero in whom the ideals of Religion and Chivalry burned with equal ardour. Wolfram's *Parsifal* is the greatest epic of the 13th century. Here at the moment when Rheims Cathedral was begun, the young knight is taught to " keep his soul pledged to God, without losing his hold on the world ". And he is taught that " in joy and in grief right measure " should always be his guide. That sounds like the Greek " Nothing in excess ", but it is not. It is just as in architecture, a balance gained as the ultimate prize by him who indefatigably strives for his redemption. A noble and upright ideal worthy of the great cathedrals and the superb sculptures of their portals. At Chartres, under the name of St. Theodore, one can see him, the knight of the Parsival virtues, standing in the porch of the South transept, and at Rheims, as an unknown king, under a canopy of one of the buttresses, and on horseback at Bamberg, and again with the most beautiful young women that Western sculptors ever carved, women both vigorous and maidenly, around the choir of Naumburg cathedral.

In England the emissaries of Henry VIII and of Cromwell have destroyed the majority of what there was of cathedral sculpture. A few pieces that are left, such as a headless figure at Winchester, are of the same character and

quality as 13th-century sculpture in France. But neither
the façade of Wells nor the surviving statues at Lincoln
and Westminster are up to the standards of Chartres and
Rheims. The English are not a sculptural race. Their
architecture, however, the style which they evolved, is just
as exquisite as that of the French cathedrals, and at the
same time typically English, known under the name of
Early English.

Originally it came from France, as did the Gothic style
in all countries. The Cistercians, the new reformed order
of the 12th century, to which St. Bernard belonged, favoured
it. Cistercian houses in England were amongst the first
to use pointed arches. Into cathedral architecture it was
introduced by William of Sens at Canterbury. Details
there are French in character. What is, however, unusual
in France, is the duplicating of the transepts as we find it at
Canterbury and then at Lincoln, Wells, Salisbury and many
more cathedrals. It is not a feature invented in England.
Cluny, the centre of the most influential Benedictine order
before the foundation of the Cistercians, had it—not in the
10th-century shape of the church which is illustrated
(fig. 6) but as it was rebuilt in 1095 seqq. (pl. VII B). The
fact that this duplication remained solitary in France but
became so popular in England is eminently characteristic of
the different approach to architecture in the two countries.
The Gothic style in France, as we have seen, tends all to
spatial concentration. The Early English style lacks that
quality. A cathedral such as Salisbury with its square East
end and its square double transepts (fig. 16) is still the sum,
as it were, of added units, compartment joined to compartment. Looking, at, say, Lincoln and then at Rheims (pl.
XIII), this difference comes out most eloquently. Rheims
seems vigorously pulled together, Lincoln comfortably
spread out. The same contrast can be found in the West
façades. The English ones are comparatively insignificant.
Porches, added to the naves and developed sometimes into
superb pieces of independent decorative architecture,
serve as main entrances instead. And where there are fully
developed façades as at Wells and Lincoln, they have an
existence unrelated to the interiors behind, are screens,

as it were, placed in front of the church proper, and not the
logically designed outward projection of the inside system,
as are French façades.   It has been said that this seemingly
conservative attitude of English architects was due to the
survival of so many big Norman cathedrals, the foundations
and walls of which were used in the rebuilding.   But this
materialistic explanation, like so many of the same kind,
does not hold good.   Salisbury was a new foundation.
There was nothing on the site when the first stone was laid
in 1220 (the same year in which Amiens Cathedral was
begun).   The preference for the " additive " ground plan
must therefore be accepted as a national peculiarity; and

Fig. 16.—Salisbury Cathedral, begun 1220.   Length *c.* 475 ft.

once one has realised that, one will recognise its essential
similarity to the Anglo-Saxon ground plans of churches such
as Bradford-on-Avon (fig. 4), and also its harmony with the
specifically national qualities in Early English elevations.

Canterbury cannot unreservedly be called English;
Wells and Lincoln are.   Wells was begun just before 1191,
Lincoln in 1192.   If one compares the nave of Lincoln
roofed in 1233 (pl. xiv A) with that of Amiens, the national
contrast is obvious.   Yet both cathedrals are of the aristo-
cratic, youthful yet disciplined, vigorous yet graceful, spirit
of the 13th century.   The bays in Lincoln are wide, while
they are narrow in Amiens, the piers are of comfortable
proportions; no shafts run right through from bottom to

top. Those supporting the ribs of the vaults rest on corbels just above the capitals of the piers—an illogical arrangement from the French point of view. The triforium gallery has broad, low openings and pointed arches, so low that they seem round—another inconsistency, a French critic would say. And most curious of all to anybody thinking in terms of Amiens or Beauvais is the vault. For while the French vault is the logical termination of the bay system, the vault of Lincoln has besides the transverse ribs separating bay from bay, and the four cross ribs, a ridge-rib running all along the centre of the vault parallel to the arcades, and so-called tiercerons, i.e., ribs springing from the same capitals as the cross ribs, but leading up to other points along the ridge or at right angles to the ridge. Thus the vault in Lincoln assumes the shape of a sequence of stars—more decorative but less reasonable than the French system.

In all this, the Early English style appears the true representative of a national character that seems scarcely changed to this day. There is still the same distrust of the consistent and logical and the extreme and uncompromising. Now it has not been possible to discover these peculiarly English qualities in Norman architecture, and it is worth mentioning in this context that just about the middle of the 13th century there are other indications as well of an awakening of national consciousness. The Provisions of Oxford of 1258 are the first official document with a text not only in French (or Latin) but also in English. And they declare that no Royal fiefs shall in future go to foreigners, and that the Commanders of Royal Castles and ports must in future all be English. It is known that Simon de Montfort's revolt was a national movement, and that Edward I was influenced by Simon's ideas to a considerable extent. The same tendency towards national differentiation can incidentally be noticed during the same period in other European countries. It may be connected with the experiences of the Crusades. Here the knights of the West, though united in a common enterprise, must for the first time have become aware of the contrasts of behaviour, feelings and customs of the nations.

As far as architecture is concerned, the Crusades have had,

beyond this, one more immediate effect. They caused a complete reform in the planning and building of castles. Instead of the Norman reliance for defence on the keep, a system of concentric curtain walls with towers at intervals was now adopted. It came from the mighty castles (such as Le Crak des Chevaliers) built by the Crusaders in Syria and the Holy Land. The Crusaders took it from the Turks, who in their turn had derived it from Roman military architecture. The Tower of London, as enlarged by Henry III and his successors, is an instance of this concentric plan. What is, however, more specially important here, is

Fig. 17.—Harlech Castle, chiefly 1286–1290.

the fact that the new functional standard is accompanied at least in a number of cases by a new æsthetic standard. To the architects who designed the Edwardian castles of Wales the appearance of the Norman castle, with its irregular bailey and its keep on a mount in one corner, was haphazard and untidy. They rediscovered symmetry as a possible planning principle for castles—re-discovered, because Rome had known it. Just as they designed newly-founded towns (New Winchelsea, e.g.), on the chessboard pattern, they ventured to make of Harlech and Beaumaris completely symmetrical configurations (fig. 17). The effect, in Harlech especially, is one of overwhelming majesty.

Far too few people know that here, in Wales, the most consummate masterpieces of European military architecture are to be found.   For grandeur and daring of conception, only the Emperor Frederic II's slightly earlier Castel del Monte in South Italy can be compared, again a synthesis of Roman, Eastern and Gothic elements.

In English religious architecture the achievement that lends itself most readily to a comparison with Harlech and Beaumaris is the 13th-century chapter house, again something specifically English, again something hardly known abroad and—owing to the British inferiority complex in matters of art—insufficiently appreciated over here.   Salisbury Chapter House of about 1275 (pl. xi) is centrally planned, an octagon with a central pillar and spacious windows filling the walls entirely except for the arcade strip just above the stone benches for the members of the Chapter.   But while in France such glass walls give a sensation of a rapturous union with a mysterious world beyond ours, the proportions of the windows at Salisbury with their generously sized tracery circles keep the interior in safe and happy contact with the ground. A sunny breadth is achieved which makes Amiens feel both over-pointed and over-excited.

At the same time the Early English style has just as much refinement, crispness and *noblesse* in every individual motif as the French style of the great cathedrals.   It is in fact this essential similarity of detail that reminds one all the time of the ultimate identity of spirit behind French and English 13th-century architecture.   To feel this, it is only necessary to look at the central pier at Salisbury or the piers of the nave arcade in Lincoln with their slender detached shafts and their resilient crocket capitals (of a type equally characteristic of *c.* 1200 in England and France, cf. fig. 18), or at the clarity and erectness of the English lancet window (English in that it presupposes a solid wall into which it is placed as against the French elimination of the whole wall), or at the masterful carving of the leaves around the capitals of Southwell Chapter House (pl. xv A) throbbing with life, yet kept under the strict discipline of architecture, economic in treatment, nowhere fussy or ostentatious, and of a precision of surface only to be compared with the classic Greek art of the Parthenon

4. Périgueux, South-west France, St. Front, *c.* 1125–50. *B.* St. Gilles, Provence. The façade, *c.* 1150.

Amiens Cathedral, begun 1220.

Salisbury Cathedral, Chapter House, *c.* 1275.

Plate XII. Rheims Cathedral, western front, begun *c.* 1225.
Plate XIII. A. Rheims Cathedral, begun 1211, choir, transepts and nave, 13th century, upper storeys of towers 15th century. *B.* Lincoln Cathedral, chiefly 1190–1280. Upper parts of towers 14th century.

A. Lincoln Cathedral, nave, roofed 1233.   *B.* Lincoln Cathedral, angel choir, begun 1256.

A. Southwell Minster, Nottinghamshire, capital from the chapter house, late 13th century.
B. Ely Cathedral, Lady Chapel, 1321–49.

A. Gloucester Cathedral, the choir, begun 1337.
B. Gloucester Cathedral, the vault of the choir.

But the Classic is only a moment in the history of a civilisation. The most progressive had reached it in France and England at the end of the 12th century. The most progressive were tired of it and embarked on new adventures shortly after the middle of the 13th. In France, however, the magnificent creative impulse soon flagged—after the

Fig. 18.—Laon Cathedral: Crocket capital, *c.* 1200.

Sainte Chapelle in Paris and the gigantic choir of Beauvais there was nothing for a long time with such intensity of life. England on the other hand kept up her creative energy for another century. In fact, the architecture of England between 1250 and 1350 was, although the English do not know it, the most forward, the most important, and the most inspired in Europe.

CHAPTER FOUR

THE LATE GOTHIC STYLE
(*c*. 1250–*c*. 1500)

LATE Gothic, though by the predominant use of the pointed arch still part of the Gothic style, is essentially different from the High Gothic of the great French cathedrals of Paris, Rheims and Amiens, and the English cathedrals of Salisbury and Lincoln. Its coming can clearly be traced within Lincoln Cathedral. The retrochoir or Angel Choir (pl. XIV B) was begun in 1256. It is of supreme beauty, but it possesses no longer the freshness of Spring or early Summer; this abundance of rich and mellow decoration has the warmth and sweetness of August and September, of harvest and vintage. But what generous fulfilment in the luxuriant foliage of the corbels and the gallery shafts and capitals, the full mouldings of the arcades and tracery of the gallery, and, above all, the two gorgeous layers of tracery up in the clerestory: one in the windows and one separating the wall-passage from the interior.

While here there is still breadth and fullness, in other equally advanced work of the same date a tendency becomes noticeable towards the more sophisticated and at the same time the more complicated. This tendency runs parallel with the dominant tendency in contemporary philosophy— the abstruse intricacies of Duns Scotus (born *c*. 1270) and his pupil Occam (died *c*. 1347)—and also with that in French architecture. But whereas the result in France is lean and reactionary, England went on inventing forms with amazing profuseness, forms merely decorative, no longer strictly architectural. The most perfect expression of this new spirit is in the kind of tracery which is called flowing as against the geometrical tracery of 1230 to about 1300. The economy of the Early English—a feature of all classic phases—is in strong contrast to the infinite variety of the Decorated. Where there had been exclusively circles with inscribed trefoils, quatrefoils, etc., there are now pointed trefoils, and ogee or double curved arches, shapes like daggers and shapes like the *vesica piscis*, and whole systems of reticulations (fig. 19).

To study this new English flow in terms of space, one must go to one West country and one East country church: the cathedral (then abbey church) of Bristol, and the cathedral of Ely. The chancel of Bristol was begun in 1298 and chiefly

Fig. 19.—Flowing tracery from Tilty Church, Essex.

built during the first third of the 14th century (pl. xix A). It differs in four significant things from all English cathedrals of the preceding period. It is an aisled hall, not a basilica— that means that its aisles are as high as its nave, so that no clerestory exists. This type of church elevation had existed in Romanesque South-Western France (see p. 41), but it had then nowhere attempted what it now does: the creation of a unified room with piers inserted, instead of the classic Gothic principle of a staggered elevation from aisle to nave. This tendency towards the unified room has its origin in the hall of castle and monastery, especially in refectories and dormitories. Its introduction into church architecture made the Bristol architects change, with a self-certainty remarkable at such an early date, the shapes of both piers and vaults. The piers, a peculiarity exceptional before the 15th century, have no capitals, the vaults no special emphasis on the transverse arches. That means that no halt stops the flow up these shafts and into the ribs, and the flow along the star-like formations of the primary and secondary ribs. There appears in this a deliberate break with the classic Gothic principle of functional articulation all the way through from pier base to vault boss. Moreover, to support the weight of the nave vault which in a basilican Gothic church is conducted down by flying buttresses to the roof of the aisles and then by buttresses to ground level, the aisles are crossed at the level of the springing of their vaults by curiously ingenious and yet naïve struts or bridges thrown across below the transverse arches. From their centres little fan vaults push up their many ribs to join the decorative system of the vault. The device may have been thought out for technical reasons: it is æsthetically most effective all the same. A classic Gothic interior is meant to affect us in two directions only: the façade-altar direction and the other, at right angles to it, which make us see the sheets of stained glass and the tracery on the right and the left. At Bristol our eyes are lured all the time into glimpses diagonally up and across.

The same effect can be studied on a larger scale in Wells Cathedral, where in 1338 an enormous arch or strut of similar design and function was placed between nave and crossing to support the crossing tower. It is grossly baffling, but undeniably impressive. At Bristol itself the cathedral architect has given a more playful version of the same spatial motifs in the sacristy of the cathedral. Here the ribs of the little vault are accompanied by a skeleton of secondary flying ribs starting at a lower level than the others, shooting through the air and meeting the primary ones at the central boss. The effect is again one of deliberate and pleasing confusion. Classic Gothic ribs, just like classic Gothic arches, keep strictly to the strata of space assigned to them; they never stray into others.

At Ely more than anywhere else the new attitude towards space has found an adequate form. Between 1322 and 1342 the crossing of the cathedral was rebuilt in the form of an octagon. The choice of this shape can have been nothing but a deliberate attempt at breaking the 13th century's discipline of right angles. The diagonal axes, with their large windows and flowing tracery, destroy the precise dividing lines between nave, aisles, transepts and choir which had been the groundwork in the plan and elevation of a classic Gothic church. It has been argued that the glass of Amiens or the Sainte Chapelle also breaks this logicality of the Earlier Middle Ages by opening the room towards a mysterious transcendental world. That is not so; the sheets of glass may give a diaphanous character to the enclosure, but it is an enclosure all the same. It doesn't really allow the eye to wander into dim, incomprehensible distances. The octagon of Ely has this very effect, an effect of surprise and ambiguity.

The Lady Chapel at Ely (1321–1349) achieved the same aim by subtler and more delicate means. The rectangular chapel isolated from the main building, as only chapter houses usually are, has all the way round an exquisite arcading with crocketed ogee arches gathered together by larger three-dimensional or nodding ogee arches (pl. xv B). Ogee-curved quatrefoils with seated figures fill the spandrels. The arches are covered with a luxuriant growth of vegetation, no longer as crisp as that of the 13th century, but with its undulations of nobbly leaves and its intricacy of minute detail at once more sophisticated and, strangely enough, more uniform in its general appearance. This is due to a treatment that makes it impossible to isolate part from part, as one could in looking at the leaves of Southwell. Now all one sees is an incessant ripple and flow, lights and shadows whisking over bossy surfaces, fascinating but far removed from the clarity of a hundred years ago.

The three-dimensional ogee-arch is a motif of great

significance. It does what the octagon does in Ely Cathedral, and the piers without capitals, the vaults without transverse arches and the bridges in the aisles did in Bristol—it sets space into a motion, quicker, more complicated and less single-minded than any to be experienced in Early English churches. Its immediate forerunner in the three-dimensional treatment of a wall is the chapter house of York Cathedral, c. 1290, where the seats around the walls have not blind arcades behind, as at Salisbury (pl. xi) about fifteen years before, but are placed into tiny polygonal niches. Their forty-four times repeated projection causes a spatial ripple too slight still to be felt as breaking the continuity of the wall, but quite noticeable, once one is aware of the coming of this new tendency.

This tendency was by no means exclusively English. Continental countries experienced it too, though considerably later. France especially did not fully wake up to the spatial and ornamental implications of the Late Gothic style until the end of the 15th century. Her " Flamboyant " is essentially nothing but a translation of English 14th-century ornament into the sharper, spikier forms of a later age. Sometimes fascinating work was achieved—at Rouen in particular, where St. Maclou, the nave of St. Ouen, and of the Cathedral the main portal, the library court and the Tour de Beurre belong to the Flamboyant—but historically speaking all this is of much less relevance than the earlier achievements of England and the contemporary achievements of Germany and Spain.

But what of Italy during the centuries of the Gothic style? As a matter of fact Italy proved almost wholly unresponsive to it in all its forms and phases. Gothic was and remained alien. It could gain universal access only after the new Orders of Preachers, the Franciscans and Dominicans (founded in 1209 and 1215), had transformed it root and branch. Most of their later 13th-century churches were, in accordance with their rules, of a simple and useful plan, plain unaisled halls, barns as it were, with nothing to suggest an ecclesiastical atmosphere but the eastern chapels. The size of some of them, e.g. those of Siena, is enormous, which makes their spatial openness even more bewildering, however much it fitted the new æsthetic desires of the coming age as well as the functional desires of Franciscans and Dominicans. At Bristol, it had been shown, the replacement of the Basilican scheme by the aisled hall tended to make the whole area of the chancel appear one room instead of a group of three with one dominant and two accompanying. The Italian abolition of the aisles was an even more drastic means to the same end. The Friars were not afraid of drastic means. They liked the strong effect on the masses. As they scorned the sheltered and leisurely life of the other Orders on their country estates, as they chose the busy towns to settle in, and as they developed the popular sermon as a medium of religious propaganda to a degree never attempted since the early days of the Crusades, so their churches were purposely designed to be preaching halls of vast dimensions and nothing else.

The parallel between the spatial effects of this attitude and the spatial adventures of Bristol and Ely may not at once seem convincing. The connecting link between the two is in some ways the Late Gothic style in Germany, since it combines the principle of the plain enclosure with that of a *Waldweben* inside. In Germany, too, the Friars were instrumental in disseminating the new style. It was however created in parish churches, and parish churches are its chief monuments, the parish churches of the 14th and 15th centuries in which, as in the Friars' churches, the sermon grew more and more to be the centre of the service. The movement away from High Gothic principles started later than in England and Italy, about 1350, and culminated as late as in France: about 1500. Its favourite vehicle was the aisled hall, an exception—in spite of Bristol—in English (and also in French) church architecture. For 14th- and 15th-century Germany it became almost a matter of course, especially in Westphalia, in the brick districts of the Hanseatic coast towns and of Bavaria, and, after the discovery of silver, in the newly founded, newly prospering towns of Upper Saxony. It had had a long national history, going back much further than the date of Bristol. There are occasional Romanesque aisled halls in Germany, even one (on a small scale) as early as 1015. It may thus not be necessary to suppose connections with the aisled halls of South-West France. Aisled halls in Gothic forms were built directly the style had been taken over. As in England, the new inspiration came probably from the refectories and chapter houses of German (chiefly Cistercian) monasteries. The type spread during the second half of the 13th century, and assumed its German characteristics: wide arcades and wide aisles. These, needless to say, invite the eye, even more than the narrower openings of Bristol, to wander off the main Gothic lines of vision. Diagonal vistas spread on all sides. Space seems to flow directionlessly around us while we walk in the church. A proof of the master builders' conscious development are the cases in which a choir in the New Late Gothic style was added without any æsthetic mediation to an earlier nave. This is for instance the case at St. Lawrence's, Nuremberg, of 1445–72 (pl. XIX B). Having walked along the nave in the rigidly prescribed way of the Romanesque or earlier Gothic basilica, the entrance into the wider and higher choir with nave and aisles of identical width comes as a startling surprise. Bays are wider, piers slenderer, vaults of a rich star-like configuration (as created by the English nearly 200 years before), weighing down the vertical push of the piers. These have no capitals (again a motif of English priority), and so the streams of energy conducted upwards flew away undammed into ribs extending in all directions.* The sculptural decoration of the choir emphasises its spatial freedom. The magnificent stone spire of the tabernacle (now, I understand, destroyed by a bomb) rises in an asymmetrical position into the vault, and the huge locket of Veit Stoss's wood-carved Annunciation hangs down, joyful and transparent, into the space in front of the altar, so that you see it against the light of the central upper window. There are two rows of windows all the way round, and this, as the close pattern of the star vault,

---

* Some of the latest and best German churches of this period (e.g., Annaberg) have octagonal piers with concave sides—a particularly clear indication of the tendency to make the space of nave and aisles surge up from all directions against the stone divisions. The same type of piers occurs in Cotswold churches (Chipping Campden). Flying ribs as in the sacristy of Bristol incidentally are also a speciality of the boldest of these Late Gothic German churches.

adds weight to the horizontals. The classic Gothic *excelsior* is effectively (and no doubt consciously) broken. The earth claims her own against heaven. The clouds of the Reformation were gathering. Luther was born before the tabernacle and the Annunciation were commissioned. The discrepancy between interiors of undulating flow, in which the individual may lose himself as between the trees of a forest, and exteriors of powerful solidity with unbroken walls and two rows of windows, heralds the mood of the German Reformation, torn between mystical introspection and a hearty new thrust into this world. Moreover, the new rooms of German Late Gothic had a practical advantage— the same as the aisleless halls of the Italian Friars: they were evidently much better suited for listening to long sermons than the old interiors with parallel and separated avenues.

However, practical considerations alone did not create the new style, nor can it be said that the spirit of the coming Reformation alone created it. For it is just as noticeable in Spain as in Germany. In Spanish architecture of the 15th century there was a good deal of German influence. Masters from Cologne and Nuremberg were called to Burgos and established such German motifs as star-vaults and net-vaults. But these masons and stone-carvers from the North would hardly have been so successful if there had not been an indigenous Spanish trend towards the new Late Gothic expression. The star-vaults seemed no more than a variation of the theme of the Mohammedan dome with its flying ribs forming stars of many kinds. The conciseness of the classic French cross-vaults and indeed classic French ideals altogether had not appealed to Spaniards. As in Germany, imitation of French Gothic is rare, and as in Germany there are wide aisles, although they are lower than the nave (that is basilican), and side chapels between the buttresses so that the exteriors seem flat and less articulated than those of the 13th century—again two clear proofs of the tendency towards one unified room (fig. 20).

This tendency is nowhere more obvious than in Catalonia, not until 1479 united with Central and Northern Spain. The typical Catalan plan of the 14th and 15th centuries is a wide aisleless or aisled hall with side-chapels between the buttresses and a very wide shallow apse. The exteriors are bare as in Germany, the interiors spacious and plain, the right kind to hold the large congregations of the prosperous trading towns of the Catalan coast. Again this practical advantage may have had something to do with the plan chosen. But it is hardly enough to explain the interesting

Fig. 20.—Juan Gil de Hontañon: Salamanca Cathedral, begun 1512.

case of Gerona Cathedral which had been begun in the French way with a choir, ambulatory and radiating chapels in 1312. When these eastern parts were complete, work for some reason stopped, and it was not until 1416 that the then master-mason Guillermo Boffiy suggested the adding of a new nave. His daring suggestion was a nave without aisles

the width of apse and ambulatory put together. There
was opposition amongst the cathedral authorities, and so—a
curiously modern idea—a Commission was appointed to
decide. Its members were twelve leading architects.
Their answers have been preserved. Seven members were
in favour of continuing the basilican scheme westward, but
five were taken with Boffiy's idea. In 1417 in fact Boffiy
was committed to start on his scheme. It is a masterpiece
of building technique, with a clear span of 73 ft., one of the
widest vaulted rooms of mediæval Europe (fig. 21). The
weight of the vaults is in the usual Spanish way carried by
internal buttresses with chapels in the interstices. The room
is somewhat bare, as the friars' churches of Tuscany, but it
has a great power, and it certainly is, with its sharp contrast
of one room in the West and a system of three spatial units
of staggered height and width in the East, the most convincing proof of the change of style from High to Late
Gothic.

But when did the one phase end and the other begin?
Our Spanish and German examples were of the 15th
century, our examples from England of the early years of
the 14th. The nave of Gerona is plain and solid, without
mystery. So are at least the exteriors of the Late Gothic
churches of Germany. Their interiors on the other hand
are full of movement, unrestrained in feeling, romantically rich and romantically vague. They share these qualities
with Bristol and Ely. Neither Bristol however nor Ely aims
at the contrast of square exterior volume and floating
interior space. Nor did Britain even at the late date of the
Nuremberg choir of St. Lawrence's go to such extremes.
Nevertheless British architectural style had changed signally
between 1300 and 1450. The change is so obvious that,
while for the Continent the terms High and Late Gothic are
sufficient to indicate the chief stages, English tradition has for
more than a hundred years preferred a division into three
Gothic phases: Early English, Decorated and Perpendicular.
Early English was at an end when the Angel Choir was
growing. Decorated is the style of Bristol and Ely. Perpendicular corresponds to what we have seen of Late
Gothic in Germany and Spain, and it is a contribution of

Fig. 21.—Guillermo Boffiy: Gerona Cathedral. The architect added to a 14th-century choir with ambulatory a nave without aisles to the width of choir and ambulatory. Begun 1417.

equal national vigour. Once it had been created by a few strong-minded, clear-headed architects, it brushed aside all the vagaries of Decorated and settled down to a long, none too adventurous development of a plain-spoken idiom, sober and wide awake. People have tried to connect the coming of this new style with the Black Death of 1349. This is wrong; for it is there in all its perfection as early as 1331 in the South transept and as early as 1337 in the choir of Gloucester Cathedral (pl. xvi). The thick circular piers of the Norman choir were left standing but with their galleries hidden behind a screen of lean uprights and horizontals divided up into rows of panels. The East wall was opened into one huge window with, except for the few main partitions, nothing but a system of glazed panels. The number of horizontal divisions invalidates all that might have been left of the upward soar of earlier Gothic architecture. In this the same new tendency is visible as in the double rows of windows in German churches. But while on the Continent the walls were made solid too, English Perpendicular walls remained glass screens. And just as thus the wall structure was less drastically changed than in Germany or Spain, so the spatial character of Perpendicular rooms returned to the clarity of earlier Gothic. Basilican plans were only very rarely given up in favour of the spatially more promising aisled hall plan of Bristol and Germany. The only fanciful feature in Gloucester and indeed in many other Perpendicular parts of cathedral and abbey churches is the decoration of the vaults (pl. xvi B). There is as much imagination displayed in them as in the German and Spanish vaults. In fact neither of these two countries, let alone France, has produced anything so complicated as the scheme of Gloucester at so early a date. On the other hand Perpendicular vault decoration is harsher than that of Continental Late Gothic, just as Perpendicular tracery is harsher than German, Spanish or French tracery of about 1500 (or than English tracery of 1320). The ribs of Gloucester form patterns as abstract and as angular as the match-sticks on the walls of Earl's Barton tower three hundred years before, patterns equally remote from the luxuriance of Ely, the resilience of Lincoln and the structural logicality of classic French rib-vaults.

Of structural logicality especially there is none in Perpendicular vaults. These close-knit patterns of ribs have no longer anything to do with vault construction. The main transverse ribs and cross ribs are no longer distinguishable from the innumerable tiercerons (i.e., ribs connecting the caps of the vault shafts with points on the ridge rib) and liernes (i.e., ribs neither springing from the vault shafts nor leading to any of the main crossings). The whole is in fact a solidly built barrel-vault with plenty of decoration applied to it. The use of the term barrel-vault implies that the effect of Perpendicular vaults is as much an emphasis on the horizontal, as it were, lid character as the star-vaults of Germany and Spain. This interpretation is confirmed by the general substitution in English Perpendicular exteriors of low-pitched, often parapeted roofs for the higher pitch of the 12th and 13th centuries.

Gloucester is the most consistent example of the Perpendicular in English cathedrals. The naves of Winchester and Canterbury (chiefly of the later 14th century) are less uncompromising. In other cathedrals the late Middle Ages did little major work. To find English architecture of 1350 to 1525 at its best, one should not visit cathedrals and abbey churches, one should go to the manor houses and parish churches for the happiest *ensembles* and to the Royal Chapels for the highest architectural standard. This change in the relative importance of buildings is due to social and historical reasons.

Taking domestic architecture first, what had happened between the age of Harlech and that of, e.g., Penshurst in Kent (pl. XVII A) begun, it seems, in 1341, is that half a century of internal peace had made owners of large houses in the country give up thoughts of military defence and allow themselves more domestic comforts. The extremely compact arrangement of rooms in the earlier castles was no longer necessary. Its essentials were kept—the hall as the centre of household life, with the high-table for the lord and his family at one end, the entrance and a screened-off gangway at the other, a parlour or chamber with perhaps a

KITCHEN
PANTRY BUTTERY
ETC.

ENTRY

LATER
PARTITIONS

GREAT HALL

7TH CENTURY
PANELLING

PARLOUR
(SOLAR OVER)

PORCH

COURT

GATEHOUSE

0   10   20   30   40   50   60   70
FEET

Fig. 22.—Cothay Manor, Somerset, late 15th century.

solar above beyond the high-table end of the hall, and
kitchen, pantry, larders, buttery, etc., on the other side of
the screens—but more rooms were added and the hall itself
was provided with larger windows of several lights and a
bay-window at the high-table end. The grandest of
surviving 14th-century halls is John of Gaunt's at Kenil-
worth, 90 by 45 feet in size. In some houses at that time a
separate dining-room must already have existed. That
appears from a passage in *Piers Plowman*. It means a first
step towards the desertion of the hall as the living-room
and dining-room of everybody, master and men. But nearly
three centuries had to pass by after Penshurst had been
designed, before the hall had finally become a vestibule and
nothing else.

It took nearly as long to recover the principle of symmetry for the English house which had governed the plans
of Harlech and Beaumaris with such splendid success. In
the 14th and 15th centuries a manor house, or, for that
matter, a French *château* and a *Burg* in Germany, were
picturesque agglomerations of rooms. Symmetry did not
go further than that sometimes in the 15th and early 16th
centuries one straight axis runs from the gate-house to the
entrance of the hall. But the hall was not the exact centre
of the main block, and its entrance was eccentric anyway.
The gate-house, even when it was in the middle of the outer
front, did not separate identical halves. The results of this
undisturbed growth are in Britain, as well as in France and
Germany, extremely charming. But if one enquires about
strictly æsthetic qualities, they are certainly not as high as
those of Harlech.

A comparison between the English cathedral of the 13th
century and the English parish church of the 15th shows the
same changes. They are largely due to social developments. A new class had come into its own, the class
responsible for the erection of the scores of splendid parish
churches in Germany and in the Netherlands, and the class
to which in France the business-minded Royal admini-
strators of the William of Nogaret type, in Italy the Medici
and their friends and competitors, and in Northern Germany
the leaders of the Hanseatic League belonged. In England

Richard the Lion-Hearted had been on the throne when Lincoln and Wells were designed, and Henry III, the Saintly King as Rome called him, ruled when Salisbury and the new Westminster Abbey were designed. Simon de Montfort stood up against Henry III, a hero of the national English cause against too papal a policy, when the Angel Choir was added to Lincoln Cathedral. Less than a hundred years later, Edward III, who was crowned in 1327 and died in 1377, accepted with pleasure the honour of membership in the London Guild of the Merchant Taylors, i.e., the cloth merchants of the City. This is an eminently revealing fact, especially if it is viewed in conjunction with commercial and industrial developments in the Netherlands, Germany, Tuscany and Catalonia. In England the age of Edward III saw a rapid development of business enterprise. Flemish weavers were called into the country, trade interests played a considerable part in the vicissitudes of the Hundred Years War. Vast capitals were accumulated by men such as Dick Whittington and John Poulteney, whose country seat was Penshurst. In fact more of the manor houses of the late Middle Ages were owned by merchants or their descendants than is usually realized. After the decimation of the old aristocracy caused by the Wars of the Roses, the proportion of *nouveaux riches* amongst the peers of the realm grew ever more rapidly, until in the council of sixteen whom Henry VIII named to reign for his little son, not one was a peer of twelve years' standing.

Thus by 1500 the most active patrons of art were the King and the towns. The Crown had, about 1330, built St. Stephen's Chapel in the Palace of Westminster which was burnt in 1834. Judging from surviving drawings it must have been a building of great artistic importance. Then in the 15th century Henry VI and VII built Eton College Chapel (begun in 1441), King's College Chapel, Cambridge (begun in 1446), Henry VII and VIII St. George's Chapel, Windsor Castle (begun in 1481), and Henry VIII the Chapel of Henry VII at the East end of Westminster Abbey (1503–1519). They are buildings of extremely simple exteriors and plans, but with plenty of masterfully executed decoration. The contrast is especially poignant at Cambridge. To design this long, tall, narrow box of a College chapel (pl. xx A), no spatial genius was needed. There is no differentiation at all between nave and choir. The decoration too is repetitive, the same window tracery is used twenty-four times, and the same panelled fan-vaulting motif. They were rationalists, the men who designed and enjoyed these buildings, proud constructors, of a boldness not inferior to that of the Catalans. Yet they succeeded—and here we are faced with the same problem as in the contemporary German churches—in combining this practical, matter-of-fact spirit with a sense of mystery and an almost oriental effusion of ornament. Standing at the West end of the nave one can hardly think of the supreme economy with which this effect of exuberance has been attained. The fan vault in particular helps, wherever it is used, to create an atmosphere of heavy luxuriance. Yet it is an eminently rational vault, a technician's invention, one is inclined to surmise. It originated from the vault designs of chapter houses and their development into the palm-like spread of bunches of ribs towards a heavily bossed ridge-rib in the choir (early 14th century) and then the nave of Exeter. That had been the spatial imagination of the Decorated at its boldest moment. Then the Perpendicular came in and systematised and solidified it all, again first at Gloucester, in the East walk of the cloisters (1357–1377). By giving all ribs the same length, the same distance from each other, and the same curvature, and by applying the ubiquitous panelling to the spandrels, the palm-vault of Exeter is converted into the fan-vault of Gloucester.

This system the King's masons used at Cambridge, men who, although at this advanced hour in the development of mediæval architecture they are sometimes already mentioned with their names in documents as surveyors of works and directors of works, were still by training and experience in the same category as Villard de Honnecourt and the masters of the English and French cathedrals. But as members of the King's household they now very gradually began to advance into the status of civil servants. This development went on into the 17th century. Not until then were the

Royal architects in France and also in England primarily civil servants.

In the 14th century a man such as Henry Yevele (died 1400) appears more as the successful London mason and contractor and distinguished member of his city guild than as a Royal architect in the modern sense. We find his name coupled in one document with Chaucer's, in another with Dick Whittington's. So we imagine him in his stately fur-lined robes (which incidentally were part of his salary from the King) in his house by St. Magnus, London Bridge, or one of his two manor-houses in Kent. Of work by him, the masonry of Westminster Hall (1394–1402) survives. Such men, dignitaries of their guilds and the fraternities to which they belonged, built the stately town-halls of England, the Netherlands and the cities of the Hanseatic League. They also built the halls of the London city companies, and they built the parish churches with their guild chapels. In designing them they felt that they were working for themselves and their equals; that was a more intimate connection between architect and building than had existed before. It gives its own peculiar atmosphere to the Late Gothic parish church. The largest of them are no less lofty than cathedrals and abbey churches. The tallest of all mediæval spires in Europe is that of Ulm Minster which is a parish church. St. Mary Redcliffe in Bristol covers a larger area than many a cathedral. Prosperous small towns such as Lavenham in Suffolk and dozens of others had parish churches in which the whole local population could assemble, and the villagers from the neighbourhood still find accommodation. York has (or had before the Second World War) twenty-one surviving mediæval churches, besides the Minster.

Where existing churches were not entirely pulled down, they were enlarged, aisles were widened, naves heightened, new aisles or chapels added to the old, and the result is the picturesque, happy-go-lucky irregularity of plan and elevation of most English parish churches. However, while such churches may reflect most truly the history of their towns from the Anglo-Saxon to the Tudor age, they do not really reflect the æsthetic vision of any one period.

What the 15th century in England desired the chief parish church of a prosperous town to look like appears in such a building as St. Nicholas, King's Lynn. The church (fig. 23) was erected as a chapel of ease from 1414 to 1419. One plan is responsible for the whole building, and that plan is as uncomplicated as those of the contemporary Royal chapels. It consists of a rectangle of 162 × 70 ft. within which are comprised nave and aisles as well as aisled chancel. There is no structural articulation between West and East parts. All that interferes with the uniformity of the outline is the tower taken over from a previous building, the porch, and the slightly projecting apse. This sturdy

Fig. 23.—St. Nicholas, King's Lynn, Norfolk, 1414–19.

plainness is in accordance with the style of the exteriors of German churches. But inside such churches as St. Nicholas, King's Lynn, or the three great parish churches of Coventry (pl. xviiB), or Holy Trinity, Hull, have nothing of the romanticism of Nuremberg. They stick to the traditional Basilican elevation, piers are thin, mouldings wiry, and tracery is of the straightforward Perpendicular type. There are no corners left in mysterious semi-darkness, nor any surprising vistas. Where the fantasy of the Late Gothic designer shows itself in the English parish church is in wooden screens and wooden roofs. An almost inconceivable profusion of screens originally divided naves from choirs, aisle chapels from nave chapels, and the many guild chapels from the public spaces. The most lavishly decorated are in Devon on the one hand, in East Anglia on the other. But the greatest glory of the English parish churches are their timber roofs (pl. XVIII), roofs constructed as boldly by the carpenter as any Gothic stone vaults by masons, and looking as intricate and technically thrilling as any configuration of flying buttresses around the East end of a cathedral. There is a variety of types: the tie-beam roof, the arch-braced roof, the hammerbeam roof (devised for Westminster Hall by Yevele's colleague, the King's master carpenter, Hugh Herland in 1380), the double hammerbeam roof and others. The most ingenious of them all is the one of the unaisled church of Needham Market looking like a whole three-aisled building hovering over our heads without any visible support from below. The continent has nothing to emulate these achievements of a ship-building nation. They are in fact strongly reminiscent of ship's keels upside down.

Such roofs add a quality of structural richness to English churches which they would otherwise lack. However even they, looked at in detail, have nothing of the elegant flow of Flamboyant ornament in France, the elaborate intricacies of German Late Gothic, or the wild luxuriance of contemporary ornament in Spain and Portugal. The lines of rafters, purlins, braces are sharp, sinewy, angular—as English as the ribs of Gloucester choir and the decoration of Earl's Barton Tower.

The briefest comparison between an English parish church or even King's College Chapel and, say, the decoration of the front of the church of St. Paul's at Valladolid (begun shortly after 1486, probably by Simon of Cologne; pl. XX B) is sufficient to realise the contrast between English restraint and Spanish extremism. Substitute the St. Lawrence portal of Strasburg Cathedral for Valladolid, and you would see Anglo-German contrasts as glaringly. It might be said that German Late Gothic decoration is as extreme as Spanish, which would not be surprising, since Germany and Spain as against France, England, Italy are the countries of the extremes in European civilisation. However, there are obvious differences be-

tween the Spanish and the German ways of decorating.
Ever since Mohammedan days Spain has had a passion for
filling large surfaces with close-knit two-dimensional
ornament. The Germans share this *horror vacui*, but there
is always a marked spatial curiosity in their ornament.
That connects German Late Gothic with German Rococo
just as the flatness and the frantic movement of the Charterhouse vestry at Granada, which dates from the middle of the
18th century (see pl. XXXII) seems heralded in the details of
the Valladolid façade. Valladolid has no dominant
motifs. The figure sculpture is petty in scale. Ogee arches
and " Tudor " arches (i.e., depressed pointed arches) follow
each other. The background is patterned from top to
bottom, and the patterns change with every string course.
There is something of a thistly undergrowth about this
ensemble which makes English Perpendicular appear strong
and pure. There can be no question which of the two
countries would open itself to Puritanism and which would
become the stronghold of Baroque Catholicism.

The high water mark, however, of Late Gothic frenzy
was reached in Portugal during the spectacularly prosperous
age of King Manuel (1495–1521). Manueline decoration
in such places as Batalha and Tomar (fig. 24) is out-
rageously rich, a rank growth of forms, sometimes taken,
it seems, from crustacean organisms, sometimes from
tropical vegetation. Much Portuguese decoration was inspired by Spain and France, but here the architecture of
India, Portuguese India, is the only parallel that comes to
mind. If this connection is real it is the first instance in
Western history of non-European influence on European
art.

However, no influence can ever act, unless the one party
is ready to receive the message of the other. If the countries
of the Pyrenean Peninsula had not already been possessed
by a passion for overdone decoration, the art of the
colonies would have remained mute to them. When the
Indies became Dutch, their style did indeed after a time begin
to influence the furniture of Holland and helped to give it its
peculiar Baroque opulence, but architects wisely kept away
from it. The Dutchmen of the 17th century could never

Fig. 24.—Tomar. Window of Chapter-House, *c.* 1520.

have made of it what the Portuguese could, at that particular moment, the moment just before the ornamental imagination of the late Middle Ages was harnessed into the Renaissance yoke.

The Renaissance on the other hand could never have been conceived in a country which had as recklessly indulged in ornamental vagaries as Spain and Portugal, or as daringly explored spatial mysteries as Germany. In Italy there thus exists no Late Gothic style at all—the most striking illustration of the fact that by the 15th century the present natural divisions of Europe were more or less established. The Romanesque style had been international though regionally sub-divided, just as the Holy Roman Empire and the Church of the 11th and 12th centuries had been international forces. Then, in the 13th century, France became a nation and created the Gothic style.

Germany went through the crisis of the Interregnum and decided on a national, as against the previous international policy. The same decision was taken at the same time in England, while in Italy a wholly different development of many small town-states set in. Gothic came into Germany, Spain, England and Italy as a French fashion. Cistercian monasteries first, and then Cologne, Burgos and León, Canterbury and Frederick II's Castel del Monte (see p. 64) followed it closely. But already in Frederick II's Italian buildings there appear purely antique pediments side by side with the novel rib-vaults of France. The appreciative treatment of Roman motifs in Frederick II's Capua Gate is unparalleled anywhere in the North, and in the South only by Nicolò Pisano's pulpits. Nicolò Pisano was the first of the great Italian sculptors, the first in whose work the Italian character dominates over international conventions. His transformation of the current style in sculpture into something more static and more harmonious was paralleled by similar transformations of Gothic architecture. The rôle of the Friars in this transformation has been mentioned. There is no *excelsior* in their wide, airy, aisleless halls. The large ones with aisles, such as S. Maria Novella and S. Croce in Florence, have such wide arcades and such shallow aisles that the static nature of the rooms is hardly disturbed. The cathedral of Florence—a cathedral, but due to the financial enterprise of the guild of the wool merchants—belongs to the same family (pl. xxi B). Its piers with their substantial bases and heavy capitals do not point upward. The uninterrupted cornice provides a strong horizontal division. The cross-vaults are dome-shaped, and clearly isolate bay from bay. Clarity is also the expression of the dark structural members against the whitewashed surfaces of walls and vaults. To the traveller coming from the North these Italian interiors of the 14th century appear spacious, restful and serene.

It was only here—this will now be appreciated—that the style of the Renaissance could be conceived, here, in the land of Roman traditions, of sun, blue sea and noble hills, of vineyards and olive plantations, of pine groves, cedars and cypress trees.

CHAPTER FIVE

RENAISSANCE AND MANNERISM
(c. 1420–c. 1600)

THE GOTHIC style was created for Suger, Abbot of St. Denis, councillor of two kings of France, the Renaissance for the merchants of Florence, bankers to the kings of Europe. It is in the atmosphere of the most prosperous of Southern trading republics that about 1420 the new style emerged. A firm such as that of the Medici had its representatives in London, in Bruges and Ghent, in Lyons and Avignon, in Milan and Venice. A Medici had been Mayor of Florence in 1296, another in 1376, yet another in 1421. In 1429 Cosimo Medici became senior partner of the firm. Just over one hundred years later another Medici was created the first Duke of Tuscany. But Cosimo, whom they called in Florence the Father of the Fatherland, and his grandson Lorenzo the Magnificent, were only citizens, not even, by any official title, the first of their city. To these and to the other princely merchants, the Pitti, the Rucellai, the Strozzi, it is due that the Renaissance was at once wholeheartedly accepted in Florence and developed with a wonderful unanimity of purpose for thirty or forty years, before other cities of Italy, let alone foreign countries, had grown to understand its meaning.

This predisposition of Tuscany cannot be explained by social conditions alone. The cities of Flanders in the 15th century were socially of quite a comparable structure; so up to a point was the City of London. Yet the style in the Netherlands was a flamboyant Late Gothic; in England it was Perpendicular. In Florence what happened was that a particular social situation coincided with a particular nature of country and people, and a particular historical tradition. The geographical and national character of the Tuscans had found its earliest expression in Etruscan art. They were again clearly noticeable in the 11th century in the crisp and graceful façade of S. Miniato (pl. XXI A) and in the 14th in the spacious, happily airy Gothic churches of S. Croce, S. Maria Novella and the Cathedral of S. Maria del Fiore (pl. xxi B). Now a flourishing trading republic will tend to worldly ideals, not to the transcendental; to the active, not to meditation; to clarity, not to the obscure. And since the climate was clear, keen and salutary, and the people's minds clear, keen and proud, it was here that the clear, proud and worldly spirit of Roman Antiquity could be re-discovered, that its contrast with Christian faith did not bar its way, that its attitude to physical beauty in the Fine Arts and beauty of proportion in architecture found an echo, that its grandeur and its humanity were understood. The fragments of the Roman past in art and literature had been there all the time, and had never been entirely forgotten. But only the 14th century reached a point that made a cult of the Antique possible. Petrarch—the first Poet Laureate of modern times, crowned on the Capitol in 1341—was a Tuscan; so was Boccaccio, so was Leonardo Bruni who translated Plato. And as the Medici honoured the philosophers and called them into their innermost circle, as they honoured the poets and wrote poetry themselves, so they regarded the artists in a spirit quite different from that of the Middle Ages. The modern conception of the artist and the respect due to his genius is again of Tuscan origin.

Seven years before Petrarch was crowned in Rome, the civic authorities responsible for the appointment of a new master-mason to the Cathedral and City of Florence decided to elect Giotto, the painter, because they were convinced that the City architect should be " a famous man " above all. So for the sole reason that they believed that " in the whole world no one better could be found in this and many other things " than Giotto, they chose him, although he was not a mason at all. Now this marks the beginning of a new period in the professional history of architecture, just as Petrarch's crowning marks a new period in the history of the social status of authors. Henceforth—this is especially characteristic of the Renaissance—great architects were not usually architects by training. And henceforth great artists were honoured and admitted into positions outside their craft simply because they were great artists. Cosimo Medici is probably the first who called a painter, in recognition of his genius, divine. Later this became the attribute universally given to Michelangelo. And he, sculptor, painter and architect, a fanatical worker and a man who never spared himself, was deeply convinced that it was his due. When he felt slighted by some of the Pope's servants in an ante-room of the Vatican, he fled from Rome, deserting his post without hesitation and leaving a message that the Pope could look for him elsewhere, if he wanted him. Leonardo da Vinci at the time when this happened evolved the theory of the ideal value of art. He endeavoured to prove that painting and architecture were of the liberal arts, not arts in the trade sense of the Middle Ages. There are two sides to this theory. It demands from the patron a new attitude towards the artist, but also from the artist a new attitude towards his work. Only the artist who approached his art in an academic spirit, that is as a seeker after law, had a right to be regarded as their equal by the scholars and authors of humanism.

Leonardo has not much to say about Antiquity. But the universal fascination of Antiquity was evidently both æsthetic and social, æsthetic in so far as the forms of Roman architecture and decoration appealed to artists and patrons of the 15th century, social in so far as the study of the Roman past was accessible to the educated only. So the artist and architect who until then had been satisfied with learning their craft from their masters and developing it according to tradition and their powers of imagination, now devoted their attention to the art of Antiquity, not only because it enchanted them but also because it conferred social distinction on them. So strongly has this revival impressed the scholars from the 16th to the 19th century that they called the whole period that of re-birth, *rinascita* or Renaissance. Early writers by using this term meant the re-birth of art and letters in quite a general sense. But in the 19th century—a century of unlimited period revival—the emphasis was laid on the imitation of Roman forms and motifs. In re-examining the works of the Renaissance today, one must however ask oneself whether the new attitude towards Antiquity is really their essential innovation.

The very first building in Renaissance forms is Brunelleschi's Foundling Hospital, begun in 1421 (pl. xxii A). Brunelleschi (1377–1446) was a goldsmith by training. Yet he had been chosen to complete the Cathedral of Florence by adding the dome over the crossing, a masterpiece of construction and of shape, distinctly Gothic in character. At the same time however he designed the Foundling façade, a work of a completely different kind, consisting of a colonnade on the ground floor with delicate Corinthian columns and wide semi-circular arches letting enough sun and warmth penetrate into the loggia, and a first floor with generously spaced, moderately-sized rectangular windows under shallow pediments corresponding exactly to the arches beneath. Medallions in coloured terracotta by della Robbia—the famous babes in swaddling clothes sold in cheap copies of all sizes by the souvenir-dealers of Forence —are placed into the spandrels of the arcade. A subtly scaled architrave divides ground floor from first floor. Now the pediments over the windows are certainly a Roman motif. So seem to be the Corinthian columns. But arches on such slender columns are really in their expression just as different from those of, say, the Colosseum as they are from any Gothic arcades. Their source is the Tuscan Proto-Renaissance of S. Miniato (pl. xxi A), i.e., the architecture of Florence in the 11th and 12th centuries, and nothing else. This is an eminently significant fact. The Tuscans, unconsciously of course, prepared themselves for the reception of the Roman style by first going back to their own Romanesque Proto-Renaissance.

The relation of Brunelleschi's churches to the past is very similar. Sto. Spirito (pl. xxii B and fig. 25) which he designed in 1435 is a basilica with round-headed arcades and a flat roof; Romanesque, one can say, in these general characteristics. The bases and capitals of the Corinthian columns on the other hand and the fragments of an entablature above are Roman, rendered with a correctness and understanding of their vigorous beauty that were beyond the power of the architects of the Proto-Renaissance. The curious niches of the aisles are also Roman, though treated in a very original way. But while the motifs mentioned so far can be traced back to the Middle Ages or Antiquity, the spatial expression created with their aid is wholly new and has all the delicacy and serenity of the early Renaissance. The nave is just twice as high as it is wide. Ground floor and clerestory are of equal height.. The aisles have square bays, again half as wide as they are high. One may not at once consciously register these elementary proportions, but they contribute no doubt to the effect of serene order which the interior produces. It is difficult to-day to imagine the enthusiasm of the Early Renaissance for such simple mathematical relations in space. One must remember in

Fig. 25.—Filippo Brunelleschi: S. Spirito, Florence, begun 1435.
Length 315 ft.

order to appreciate it that at that very moment—about 1425 —painters in Florence discovered the laws of perspective. Just as they had no longer been satisfied with an arbitrary presentation of the space inside their pictures, so architects were now anxious to find rational proportions for their buildings. The effort of the 15th century to master space is only comparable with that of our own age, although that of the Renaissance concerned an ideal world and ours a material. The invention of printing towards the middle of the century proved a most powerful conquest of space. The discovery of America towards its end produced results nearly as important. Both must be named with the discovery of perspective as aspects of the Western attitude towards space, an attitude utterly alien to Antiquity, and one to which attention has already been drawn more than once in this book.

The feature of Sto. Spirito most important in this connection is the ground plan of its Eastern parts. For here Brunelleschi has departed decisively from the normal composition of Romanesque or Gothic churches. The way in which he made the transepts exactly identical with the choir, ran an aisle round all three, and placed a dome over the crossing makes us feel, looking Eastward, as if we were in a centrally planned building, a type usual in Roman architecture, both religious and secular, but very rare in mediæval Christian churches.

This could not be otherwise. For the prime function of the mediæval church was to lead the faithful to the altar. In a completely centralized building (fig. 26) no such movement is possible, and in fact no movement at all. The building has its full effect only when it is looked at from the one focal point. There the spectator must stand, and by standing there, he becomes himself " the measure of all things ". The religious meaning of the church is replaced by a human one. Man is in the church no longer pressing forward to reach a transcendental goal, but enjoying the beauty that surrounds him and the glorious sensation of being the centre of this beauty.

No more telling symbol could have been conceived for the new attitude of the humanists and their patrons to Man and religion. Pico della Mirandola, one of the most interesting of the philosophers round Lorenzo the Magnificent, delivered an address in 1486 on *The Dignity of Man*. Machiavelli, a little later, wrote his book *The Prince* to glorify the power of Man's will, and set it as the prime moving force against the powers of religion that had up to his time interfered with practical thought. And again a little later Count Castiglione composed his *Courtier* to show his contemporaries their ideal of universal man. The courtier, he says, should be agreeable in his manners, graceful, a good *causeur* and a good dancer, yet strong and fit, well versed in the pursuits of chivalry, riding, fencing and jousting. At the same time he should read poetry and history, be acquainted with Plato and Aristotle, understand all the arts, and practise music and drawing. Leonardo da Vinci was the first amongst artists to live up to this ideal: painter, architect, engineer and musician, one of the most ingenious scientists of his time, and enchanting in his personal ways. Only Christianity apparently did not occupy his mind at all. Lorenzo Valla, a Roman humanist, somewhat earlier had published his dialogue *De voluptate*, in which he openly praised the pleasures of the senses. The same Valla proved with a philological sagacity unknown before the rise of Humanism that the so-called Donation of

Fig. 26.—Leone Battista Alberti: S. Sebastiano, Mantua, begun 1460. Width inside *c.* 90 ft.

Constantine, the document on which all papal claims to worldly domination rested, was faked. Yet he died a Canon of the Lateran Cathedral in Rome. The philosophers of Florence founded an academy on Plato's model, kept Plato's supposed birthday as a holiday and preached a semi-Greek, semi-Christian religion in which Christ's love is mixed up with Plato's principle of divine love that makes us pine for beauty of soul and body in human beings. On one of the frescoes in the choir of Sta. Maria Novella an inscription can be read stating that the frescoes were completed in 1490, " when this loveliest of lands distinguished in riches, victories, arts and buildings enjoyed plenty, health and peace ". About the same time Lorenzo the Mag-

A. Penshurst Place, Kent, begun *c*. 1341.   *B*. Coventry, St. Michael's, raised to cathedral status in 1918 and destroyed by bombs in 1940.

Swaffham, Norfolk, 1474.

A. Bristol Cathedral, choir aisle, 1298–1332. *B.* Nuremberg, St. Lawrence's, 1445–72.

A. Cambridge, King's College Chapel, begun in 1446. *B.* Valladolid, St. Paul's, *c.* 1490–1515. Designed

A. Florence, S. Miniato al Monte, second half 11th century. *B.* Florence Cathedral, begun 1296, built chiefly from 1357 onwards. Principal architects: Arnolfo di Cambio, Francesco Talenti.

A. Filippo Brunelleschi : Foundling Hospital, Florence, begun 1421
B. Filippo Brunelleschi : Sto. Spirito, begun 1435.

A. Leone Battista Alberti : S. Francesco, Rimini, begun 1446. *B.* Donato Bramante : The *Tempietto* by S. Pietro in Vincoli, Rome, 1502.

A. Leone Battista Alberti: 'Palazzo Rucellai, Florence, c. 1446–51.   *B.* Raphael? : Palazzo Vidoni Caffarelli, Rome, c. 1515–20.

nificent wrote his most famous poem, which begins as follows:

> Quant'è bella giovinezza
> Che si fugge tuttavia.
> Chi vuol esser lieto sia.
> Di doman' non c' é certezza.

The lines are well known, and rightly so. They are here quoted in Italian, because they should be remembered in all their original melodiousness. Literally translated they mean:

> How lovely is youth.
> But it flies from us.
> If you want to be happy, be happy now.
> There is no certainty of to-morrow.

Now these men, if they built a church, did not want to be reminded by its appearance of that uncertain to-morrow and of what may come after this life has ended. They wanted architecture to eternalise the present. So they created the central plan for churches just as they created— at least on paper—the central plan for ideal cities (Filarete's *Sforzinda* of about 1455–60 is a regular octagon with palace and cathedral on the square in the middle). A central church, to interpret its emotional effect, is a church in which you stand still, and which stands still around you. The central plan became the ideal plan of the Renaissance, not frequent as against longitudinal buildings, but of the highest significance, wherever it appears. Brunelleschi was the first to adopt it (S. Maria degli Angeli). Alberti, of whom more will be said presently, then brought it into the most characteristic Italian shape, the Greek cross (fig. 26: S. Sebastiano, Mantua), and then, towards the end of the 15th and the beginning of the 16th century, other architects repeated and modified it, introducing, e.g., the Greek cross with apses on all ends (fig. 27), or the square with inscribed Greek cross, its cupola resting on columns.

In Leone Battista Alberti (1404–72), also a Tuscan, we find again a new type of architect. Brunelleschi and Michelangelo are sculptor-architects, Giotto and Leonardo da Vinci painter-architects. • Alberti is the first of the great dilettante-architects, a man of noble birth who first took an interest in art and architecture in the way Count Castiglione demands it from the educated courtier. He wrote a book on painting and one on the art of building (in Latin), and he spent years in Rome studying the ruins of Antiquity. It is obvious that directly the essence of architecture was considered to be philosophy and mathematics (the divine laws of order and proportion) and archeology (the monuments of Antiquity) the theoretician and dilettante would assume a new significance. Roman architecture, both system and details, must be studied and drawn to be learnt; and the

Fig. 27.—Cola da Caprarola (?), Madonna della Consolazione, Todi, begun 1508. Inner width *c*. 125 ft.

system behind the styles of Antiquity was soon—with the help of Vitruvius, the newly re-discovered Roman writer on architecture—found to lie in the orders, i.e., the proportions belonging to the Doric, Ionic, Corinthian, Composite and Tuscan columns and entablatures. By means of books on the orders foreign countries were taught the rules of classical building.

But Alberti was not a dry theorist. In him the spirit of the scholar lived in a rare and happy union with genuine imaginative and creative powers. The front of S. Francesco in Rimini (pl. XXIII A), begun in 1446 but never completed, is the first in Europe to adapt the composition of the Roman triumphal arch to church architecture. So Alberti was much more serious than Brunelleschi in reviving the

Antique. And he did not confine himself to motifs. The side of the church, opened in seven round-headed niches with heavy piers dividing them, has perhaps more of the gravity of Flavian Rome than any other building of the 15th century. Now these niches hold sarcophagi, the monuments to the humanists of Sigismondo Malatesta's court. Sigismondo Malatesta was a typical Renaissance tyrant, ruler of one of the many small Italian States, unscrupulous and cruel, but sincerely fascinated by the new learning and the new art. The church of S. Francesco was known under the name of the Temple of the Malatesta; and his intention in re-modelling it was avowedly self-glory. Across the façade an inscription runs in large letters giving Sigismondo's name and the date—nothing else.

And exactly the same pride is exhibited by Giovanni Rucellai, a merchant of Florence for whom Alberti designed the second of his church fronts. Again his name appears over-conspicuously on the façade of S. Maria Novella, and when in his old age he wrote an account of his life he said of the architectural and decorative work he had commissioned for the churches of his beloved native town: " All these things have given me, and are giving me, the greatest satisfaction and the sweetest feelings. For they do honour to the Lord, to Florence and to my own memory." It is this attitude that made it possible for the donors of the frescoes inside the choir of the same church to appear lifesize in the costumes of the day as actors in the sacred stories represented. It is this attitude also that made the patricians of Florence—and the cardinals of Rome—build their Renaissance palaces. That of the Medici begun in 1444 was the first, those of the Pitti, considerably enlarged a century later, and the Strozzi are the most famous. They are massive yet orderly, faced with heavily rusticated blocks and crowned by bold cornices. Their windows, symmetrically placed—this had not been so in the Gothic centuries—are divided into two by graceful columns (a Romanesque motif again). What one expects of Renaissance delicacy and articulation is to be found chiefly in their inner courtyards. There the ground floors are opened as cloisters with the graceful arcades of the Foundling Hospital and Sto. Spirito, and the upper floors are also enlivened by an open gallery, or pilasters dividing the walls into separate bays, or some such feature.

The first architect to transfer this principle of articulation to the palace front was again Alberti. His Palazzo Rucellai (pl. XXIV A)—built between 1446 and 1451 for the same patron as the façade of S. Maria Novella—has a much more restrained rustication, which was necessary to harmonise it with the three superimposed orders of pilasters introduced by Alberti: an equally free Ionic treatment on the ground floor, a free Doric on the first floor, and Corinthian on the top. While these pilasters articulate the front into vertical bays, sensitively designed cornices emphasise the horizontal divisions. The windows are bipartite as in the older palaces, but an architrave separates the main rectangle from the two round heads. The relation of height to width in the rectangular parts of the windows is equal to the relation of height to width in the bays. Thus the position of every detail seems to be determined. No shifting is possible. In this lies, according to Alberti's theoretical writings, the very essence of beauty, which he defines as " the harmony and concord of all the parts achieved in such a manner that nothing could be added or taken away or altered except for the worse ".

Such definitions make one feel the contrast of Renaissance and Gothic most sharply. In Gothic architecture the sensation of growth is predominant everywhere. The height of piers is not ruled by the width of bays, nor the depth of a capital or rather a cap by the height of the pier. The addition of chapels or even aisles to parish churches is much less likely to spoil the whole than in a Renaissance building. For in the Gothic style motif follows motif, as branch follows branch up a tree.

One could not imagine a donor in the 14th century decreeing, as Pope Pius II did when rebuilding the Cathedral of his native town (renamed Pienza to perpetuate his name), that no one should ever erect sepulchral monuments in the church or found new altars, or have wall-paintings executed, or add chapels, or alter the colour of walls or piers. For a Gothic building is never complete in that sense. It remains a live being influenced in its destiny by the piety of generation after generation. And as its beginning and end are not fixed in time so they are not in space. In the Renaissance style the building is an æsthetic whole consisting of self-sufficient parts. A composition in the flat or in space is arrived at by grouping such parts according to a static system.

Now the Romanesque style is—as has been shown—also a static style. It is also a style in which the adding of clearly defined spatial units is essential. How then can the difference in principle be formulated between a Norman and a Renaissance church? Walls are equally important in both, whereas the Gothic style always endeavours to invalidate them. But a Romanesque wall is primarily inert. If it is ornamented, the exact place where decoration is applied seems arbitrary. One hardly ever feels that a little more or a little less ornament, or ornament shifted to a slightly higher or slightly lower position, would make a decisive difference. In the Renaissance building this is not so. The walls appear active, enlivened by the decorative elements which in their sizes and arrangement follow laws of human reasoning. It is ultimately this humanising that makes a Renaissance building what it is. Arcades are airier and more open than they had been. The graceful columns have the beauty of animate beings. They keep to a human scale too, and as they lead from part to part, even when a building is very large, one is never overwhelmed by its sheer size. This on the other hand is just what the Norman architect wished to achieve. He conceives a wall as a whole and then keeps the expression of might and mass to the smallest detail. Hence, one need scarcely add, Romanesque sculptors could not yet re-discover the beauty of the human body. This re-discovery, and the discovery of linear perspective, had to come with the Renaissance. S. Spirito, or the Palazzo Rucellai, prove this to anyone susceptible to their specific character.

To illustrate the principle of an all-pervading order which Alberti postulates in an interior as well, the plan of S. Andrea in Mantua (begun in 1470) may be analysed (fig. 28). As in Sto. Spirito the East parts are a central composition.

One should remember that Alberti was the first to design a Renaissance church on the scheme of the Greek cross. By the addition of a nave the composition here becomes more complex. Alberti has replaced the traditional nave and aisles arrangement by a series of side chapels taking the place of the aisles and connected with the nave alternately by tall and wide and low and narrow openings. The aisles thus cease to be part of the eastward movement and become a series of minor centres accompanying the spacious barrel-vaulted nave. As to the walls enclosing the nave the same intention is evident in the replacement of the simple basilican

Fig. 28.—Leone Battista Alberti: S. Andrea, Mantua, begun 1470. Length inside c. 300 ft.

sequence of columns following each other without cæsura, by the rhythmical alteration on the *a b a* principle of the closed and the open bays. To what extent the keeping of the same proportions throughout is responsible for the deeply restful harmony of S. Andrea, will be appreciated, if one realises that the same *a b a* rhythm, identical even in details, is used as the chief motif of the façade of the church, and that the proportion of the arches of the crossing repeats that of the side chapels.

Fifty years later one architect extended this rhythmical principle of wall composition to the spatial grouping of the whole interior. In S. Salvatore in Venice designed by Spavento in 1506 (fig. 29) the nave consists of two units exactly identical with the crossing. Each unit is a Greek cross with a dome in the centre, shallow arms, and lower, also domed corner chapels. Their proportions are those of the centres. So far the system is consistent to the extreme. One feels doubtful however as to Spavento's ability to invent such a classic solution himself, if one looks at the awkward way in which the transepts and apses are attached to the body of the church.

S. Salvatore as the classic longitudinal church stands in a similar relation to S. Andrea as the Cancelleria in Rome (fig. 30) to the Palazzo Rucellai. It was built in 1486–98 as the private residence of Cardinal Riario, nephew of Sixtus IV, one of the most formidable of the Renaissance popes.

Fig. 29.—Giorgio Spavento: S. Salvatore, Venice, begun 1506. Length inside *c.* 190 ft.

They considered themselves worldly rulers almost more than priests. Julius II, another nephew of Sixtus IV, under whom the new St. Peter's was begun, and for whom Michelangelo painted the Sistine Chapel and Raphael the *Stanze* of the Vatican, asked Michelangelo to portray him in a statue for Bologna with a sword instead of a book; for, he said: "I am a soldier, not a scholar". Of Alexander VI, and his nephew Cesare Borgia, it is sufficient to mention the names in this connection. The Palazzo Riario has a ground floor without pilasters, because it seemed more reasonable to preserve the integrity of the rustication, where only small windows were required. On the first and second floors there are pilasters, but not in the simple sequence of the Palazzo Rucellai. Again the *a b a* rhythm is used to give life and rule to the façade. It will also be noticed that, whereas Alberti's horizontal divisions had to serve as cornices and at the same time window cills, the unknown architect of the Cancelleria gives each function its clearly

Fig. 30.—The Chancery Palace (Palazzo della Cancelleria) in Rome, 1486–1498.

visible architectural expression. Moreover the corner bays of the building are slightly projected, so that to the right and the left there is no vagueness about the composition either.

The Cancelleria is the first Renaissance building of more than local importance in Rome. About the time, however, when it was completed, Rome took the leadership in architecture and art out of the hands of Florence. This moment marks the beginning of the High Renaissance. The Early Renaissance was essentially Tuscan. The High Renaissance is Roman, because Rome was at that time the only international centre of civilisation, and the High Renaissance has an ideal classicity which made it internationally acceptable and in fact internationally canonic for centuries. Rome's place in the history of the Renaissance style corresponds exactly to that of Paris and the cathedrals around Paris in the history of the Gothic style. We do not know to what part of France the architects of Notre Dame, Chartres, Rheims and Amiens belonged by birth and upbringing, but we do know that Donato Bramante came from Lombardy, Raphael from Umbria, and Michelangelo from Tuscany. These are the three greatest architects of the High Renaissance, and none of them—again the case we have met before—was an architect by training. Bramante was originally a painter, Raphael too, and Michelangelo a sculptor.

Bramante was the oldest of them (1444–1514). He built in Milan in a lighthearted and extremely spirited Early Renaissance way, before the ingenious plans of Leonardo da Vinci—who lived in Milan from 1482 to 1499—made him change his style. Leonardo's architectural designs are brimful of ideas, but were done on paper only, in a semi-theoretical, as it were experimental, way to try out possibilities and develop them to their logical ends. What Leonardo's inspiration had begun in Bramante's mind, the study of the architecture of the Romans completed. Bramante's first known building in Rome, the so-called Tempietto in the courtyard of S. Pietro in Montorio (1502), is the first monument of High Renaissance architecture, truly a monument, i.e., more a sculptural than a strictly architectural achievement (pl. XXIII B). It was built to mark the spot on which St. Peter was supposed to have been crucified. One can thus call it an enlarged reliquary. In fact the intention had been to alter the courtyard in which it stood into a circular cloister to house the little temple. The first impression of the Tempietto after the churches and palaces of the 15th century is one of austerity. The order of the colonnade is Tuscan Doric, the earliest modern use of this severe, unadorned order. It supports a correct classical entablature, not roundheaded arches—again a feature that adds weight and strictness. There is moreover, except for the metopes and the shells in the niches, not a square inch of decoration on the whole of the exterior. This in conjunction with the less novel but equally telling simplicity of the proportions—the ratio between width and height of the ground floor is repeated in the upper floor—gives the Tempietto a dignity far beyond its size. Here for once the classic Renaissance has achieved its conscious aim to emulate classic Antiquity. For here is—beyond motifs and even beyond formal expression—a building that appears as nearly pure volume as a Greek temple. Space—that all-important ingredient of Western architecture—seems here defeated.

But Bramante did not stop there. Only four years after he had accomplished the ideal Renaissance expression of architectural volume, he set out to reconcile it with the ideal Renaissance expression of space, as it had been evolved by the 15th-century architects from Brunelleschi to Leonardo da Vinci. In 1506 Julius II commissioned him to rebuild St. Peter's, the holiest of Western churches. It was to be a building on a strictly central plan, an amazing decision, considering the strength of the tradition in favour of longitudinal churches on the one side and the immense religious significance of St. Peter's on the other. With the Pope adopting this symbol of worldliness for his own church, the spirit of Humanism had indeed penetrated into the innermost fortress of Christian resistance.

Bramante was over sixty when he designed St. Peter's (fig. 31), a mature work and the summing-up of all that the architects of the 15th century had pursued. It is a Greek cross, with four apses like the church at Todi (fig. 27), but so extremely symmetrical that on the plan nothing indicates which of the apses was to hold the high altar. It was to have the *a b a* rhythm in that, as at S. Salvatore in Venice, the main cupola was accompanied by minor cupolas over

corner chapels.   But the rhythm is amplified once more by
enlarging the corner chapels into Greek crosses so that each
of them has two apses of its own, the other two being cut
off by the arms of the major Greek cross.   Thus a square
ambulatory is created framing the huge central dome,
designed to be semi-spherical like the dome over the Tempietto.   Four corner turrets are added to finish the diagonal
axes and complete the exterior into a square with projec-

Fig. 31.—Donato Bramante: Original plan for St. Peter's in Rome,
1506.   Width *c.* 550 ft.

tions only for the main apses.   So far Bramante's scheme
was not more than a magnificent development of 15th-
century ideas.   What is new and entirely of the 16th
century is the modelling of the walls and above all the piers
supporting the central dome, the only parts of Bramante's
plan that were executed and still stand.   In them nothing
is left of the human scale and gentle modelling of Early
Renaissance members.   They are massive pieces of masonry,

boldly hollowed out as if by the sculptor's moulding hand. This conception of the plastic potentialities of a wall, in its origin Late Roman, was to be of the greatest importance for the future development of Italian architecture.

The immediate future however belonged to Bramante, the master of classic harmony and greatness, not to Bramante, the herald of the Baroque. Raphael (1483–1520) was the architect to follow most closely the Bramante of the Tempietto and the new courts of the Vatican (1503 seqq.), his other Roman masterpiece. Of Raphael's architectural works few are actually documented. Amongst the buildings attributed to him on good evidence is the Palazzo Vidoni Caffarelli in Rome (pl. xxiv B). The house was left incomplete and at a later date enlarged in width and height. Here again the change of scale is noticeable which marks the High Renaissance. Balance and harmony are still the aims, but they are now combined with a solemnity and greatness unknown to the 15th century. Tuscan Doric columns replace the pilasters of the Palazzo Rucellai and the Cancelleria, and the happy *a b a* rhythm is contracted into a weightier *a b* with a new accent on the *a* by the duplication of the columns, and on the *b* by the straight architraves over the windows. The rustication on the ground floor also emphasises the horizontality, i.e., the gravity of the composition.

The development from the Early to the High Renaissance, from delicacy to greatness and from a subtle planning of surfaces to a bold high relief in the modelling of walls encouraged an intensified study of the remains of Imperial Rome. The interpretation of Antiquity by the architects of the 15th century had been essentially idyllic; only now the drama of Roman architecture was seen. Only now humanists and artists endeavoured to visualise and perhaps re-create the Rome of the ruins as a whole. It is thus more than a coincidence that Raphael was appointed by Leo X, the Medici pope, in 1515 to be Superintendent of Roman Antiquities, that he had Vitruvius translated by a humanist friend for his private use, and that he (or in all probability he) drew up a memorandum to the Pope advocating the exact measuring of Roman remains, with ground plans, elevations and sections separate, and the restoration of such buildings as could be " *infallibilmente* " restored.

Here precisely archæology in the academic sense begins, an attitude quite different from that of the 15th-century admirers of Roman architecture. It produced scholars of ever wider knowledge and ever deeper appreciation of Antiquity, but artists of weakened self-confidence, classicists where Bramante and Raphael had been classics.

At this point a warning must be sounded against confusion between the three terms classic, classical and classicist. The difference between classic and classical has been pointed out on p. 41. If classic is the term denoting that rare balance of conflicting forces which marks the summit of any movement in art, and if classical is the term for anything belonging to or derived from Antiquity, what then is classicist? A definition is far from easy. In our context it can be arrived at only in a somewhat roundabout way.

Neither classic nor classical nor classicist are terms which signify historic styles such as Romanesque, Gothic and Renaissance. They coincide rather with æsthetic attitudes. However, in so far as æsthetic attitudes as a rule change with historic styles, the two sets of terms can often be co-ordinated. In England the position until a relatively short time ago was that the term Renaissance was used to cover the art from the 15th right to the early 19th century. But there had been so many fundamental changes of styles during these more than three hundred years, that the term covering such a long period could not stand for any distinct æsthetic characteristics. Thus, on the example of the Continent, it was gradually divided up into Renaissance and Baroque, the Baroque to cover the work of such artists as Bernini, Rembrandt, Velasquez. However, since our knowledge of, and susceptibility to, distinctions in æsthetic expression has grown considerably within the last fifty years or so, it is becoming more and more patent that Renaissance and Baroque do not really define the qualities of all art of importance in the 15th, 16th and 17th centuries. The contrast between Raphael and Bernini or Rembrandt is evident, but art of the period between roughly 1520 or 1530 and 1600 or 1620 does not fit into the categories of the Renaissance or the Baroque. So a new name was introduced about twenty or twenty-five years ago, Mannerism, a name which was not specially coined, but which in a derogatory sense had already been used to characterise certain schools of 16th-century painting. The name in its new sense is only now becoming known in this country. It has much to recommend it. It certainly helps to make one see the important differences between art of the High Renaissance and art of the later 16th century.

If balance and harmony are the chief characteristics of the High Renaissance, Mannerism is its very reverse; for it is an unbalanced, discordant art—now emotional to distortion (Tintoretto, El Greco), now disciplined to self-effacement (Bronzino). The High Renaissance is full, Mannerism is meagre. There is luxuriant beauty in Titian, stately gravity in Raphael and gigantic strength in Michelangelo, but Mannerist types are slim, elegant and of a stiff and highly self-conscious deportment. Self-consciousness to this extent was a new experience to the West. The Middle Ages, and the Renaissance too, had been much more naïve. Reformation and Counter-Reformation broke up that state of innocence, and this is why Mannerism is indeed full of mannerisms. For the artist now for the first time was aware of the virtues of eclecticism. Raphael and Michelangelo were recognised as the masters of a Golden Age equal to the Ancients. Imitation became a necessity, in quite a new sense. The mediæval artist had imitated his masters as a matter of course, but he had not doubted his own (or his time's) ability to surpass them. This confidence had now gone. The first Academies were founded, and a literature on the history and theory of art sprang up. Vasari is its most famous representative. Deviation from the canons of Michelangelo and Raphael was not ostracised, but it assumed a new air of the capricious, or the demonstrative, or the daring: forbidden pleasures. No wonder that the 16th century has seen the sternest ascetics and the first writers and draughtsmen to indulge in the hidden sins of pornography (Aretino and Giulio Romano).

So far only names of painters have been mentioned because the qualities of 16th-century painting are at least a little more familiar than those of architecture. The application of the principles of Mannerism to architecture is only in its very tentative stages on the Continent and in America; in England it has not even been attempted. Yet if we now turn to buildings and compare the Palazzo Farnese (fig. 32 and pl. xxviii B) with the Palazzo Massimi alle Colonne (pl. xxv A) as the most perfect examples of High Renaissance and Mannerist palace architecture in Rome, the contrast between their emotional qualities will at once be visible. The Palazzo Farnese was designed in 1530 by Antonio da San Gallo the Younger (1485–1546). It is the most monumental of Roman Renaissance palaces, an isolated rectangle of about 150 feet frontage, facing a square. The façade has strongly emphasised quoins, but no rustication. The ground-floor windows are provided with straight cornices, those on the first floor with alternating triangular and segmental pediments, supported by columns (i.e., so-called *ædiculæ*), a Roman motif revived during the High Renaissance. The top floor and the overpowering top cornice were added later and in a different spirit (see p. 122). The symmetry and spaciousness of the interior is worth noting, especially the magnificent central entrance with the barrel-vaulted passage leading into the courtyard. This (pl. xxviii B) possesses the cloistered ground floor of all Renaissance palaces, now, in accordance with the Bramante tradition, with Tuscan Doric columns and a correct frieze of metopes and triglyphs instead of the light columns of the Tuscan 15th century. The first floor has no gallery, but noble, pedimented windows set into blank arcades, and an Ionic order. This is correct according to Roman usage (Theatre of Marcellus): the sturdier Tuscan Doric must be on the ground floor, the elegant Ionic on the first, and the rich Corinthian on the second. In this (but only in this) the later second floor of the Palazzo Farnese follows the archeological example.

The Palazzo Massimi by Raphael's pupil Baldassare Peruzzi (1481–1536), begun in 1535, disregards all canons of the Ancients. Nor does it really show much regard for the achievements of Bramante and Raphael. Both the Palazzi Vidoni and Farnese were logical structures in which the knowledge of any one part gives a clue to the whole. The entrance loggia of the Palazzo Massimi with its coupled Tuscan Doric columns and its heavy cornice is in no way a

Fig. 32.—Antonio da San Gallo: Palazzo Farnese, Rome, begun 1530.

preparation for the upper floors.   Both the Palazzi Vidoni and Farnese are modelled into a generous though not over-charged relief.   In the Palazzo Massimi there is a poignant contrast between the deep darkness of the ground-floor loggia and the papery thinness and flatness of the upper parts.   The first-floor windows are shallow in relief com-pared with what the High Renaissance regarded as appro-. priate, the second and third floor windows are small and have curious leathery surrounds.   They are in no way differentiated in size or importance, as the Renaissance would have done.   Moreover a slight curve of the whole façade gives it a swaying delicacy, whereas the squareness of the Renaissance front seemed to express powerful solidity.   The Palazzo Massimi is no doubt inferior to the Palazzi Vidoni and Farnese in dignity and grandeur ; but it has a sophisticated elegance instead which appeals to the over-civilised and intellectual connoisseur.

Now this brings us back to the fact that classicism is an æsthetic attitude first appreciated during this phase of Mannerism.   The Early Renaissance had re-discovered Antiquity and enjoyed a mixture of detail copying and a naïve licence in the reconstruction of more than details. The High Renaissance was in their use of Roman forms hardly more accurate, but the Antique spirit was for a brief moment truly revived in the gravity of mature Bramante and Raphael.   After their death imitation began to freeze up initiative.   Classicism is imitation of Antiquity and even more the classic moment of the Renaissance, at the expense of direct expression.   The attitude culminated, needless to say, during the late 18th and early 19th centuries, in that phase of classicism *par excellence* which is on the Continent often called Classicism pure and simple, but which in England goes under the name of Classic Revival. The idea of copying a whole Antique temple exterior (or a whole temple front) for Western use is the quintessence of classicism.   The 16th century did not go quite so far.   But it did conceive that blend of academic rigidity with distrust of emotional freedom which made the latter-day all-out revival possible.

Another pupil of Raphael, Giulio Romano (1494–1546),

artist-in-chief to the Duke of Mantua, designed a house for himself about 1544 (pl. xxv B). It is a striking example of Mannerist classicism—apart from being one of the earliest architect's houses on such an ambitious scale. The façade is again flatter than would have pleased the High Renaissance. Detail, e.g., in the window surrounds and the top frieze, is hard and crisp. There is a proud aloofness, an almost arrogant taciturnity and a stiff formality about the building that reminds one at once of the Spanish etiquette accepted everywhere in the later 16th century. Yet the apparent general correctness is broken by an occasional, as it were, surreptitious licence here and there (one such licence in Giulio Romano's work as a draughtsman has been mentioned before). The smooth band above the windows of the rusticated ground floor seems to disappear behind the keystones of the windows. The entrance has a most illicit depressed arch, and the pediment on top with no base to it is nothing but the main string course at cill height of the first-floor windows lifted up by the effort of the arch. These windows themselves are recessed in blank arcades like those of the Palazzo Farnese, but as against the logical and structurally satisfying surrounds and pediments there, one flat ornamental motif runs without hiatus along sides, top and pediments. It is exquisite, but very self-conscious, just like the contemporary sculpture of Benvenuto Cellini.

This style, first conceived in Rome and Florence, appealed almost at once to North Italy and the transalpine countries. Giulio Romano was the first to show it north of the Apennines. Sammicheli, though fifteen years older, followed, partly under direct Roman influence, partly under the influence of Giulio's early Mantuan masterpiece, the Palazzo del Té of 1525–1535, and reshaped the appearance of Verona in this spirit of Mannerist classicism. At Bologna Sebastiano Serlio, a pupil of Peruzzi, though six years his senior, and twenty-four years older than Giulio, preached it. In 1537 he began to publish a first part of a treatise on architecture which proved a source of lasting inspiration to classicist minds the other side of the Alps. Serlio himself went to France in 1540 and was almost at once made " peintre et architecteur du roi ". The so-called school of

Fontainebleau, where Serlio and the Italians Primaticcio and Niccolò dell'Abbate worked, is the transalpine centre of Mannerism. Spain accepted the new style even earlier—a violent reaction against the violence of her Late Gothic. Charles V's new and never finished palace on the Alhambra at Granada (begun in 1526 by Pedro Machuca) looks, with its vast circular colonnaded inner court and the motifs of its 207 ft.-long façade, as though it were based on Giulio, somewhat provincially interpreted. England and Germany were slower in succumbing to the dictatorship of classicism. The style was not in all its implications appreciated before the second decade of the 17th century (Inigo Jones, see p. 180, and Elias Holl of Augsburg), and then not so much in its problematical Giulio Romano–Serlio form as in that created by the happiest and most serene of all later 16th-century artists, by Andrea Palladio (1518–1580).

Palladio's style, though it first followed Giulio, Sammicheli and Serlio, and as far as possible Vitruvius, the obscure and freely misinterpreted Roman authority on architecture, is highly personal. His work must be seen at and around Vicenza. He designed no churches there (though his San Giorgio Maggiore and Il Redentore in Venice are amongst the few really relevant churches in the Mannerist style). What he was called upon to do was almost exclusively the designing of town and country houses, *palazzi* and *ville*, and it is significant that, to show the far-reaching effect of his style, analyses of his Venetian churches can be omitted. For from the Renaissance onwards secular architecture became as important for visual self-expression as religious architecture, until during the 18th century the ascendancy of domestic and public buildings over churches was established. For the Middle Ages, in a book such as the present, it was sufficient to mention one Norman castle, one Gothic castle, and one Gothic manor house. As to the Renaissance examples so far discussed, half of them were secular. This will remain the proportion for the next two hundred years in the Roman Catholic countries. In those converted to Protestantism secular architecture was dominant at an even earlier date.

Palladio's buildings, despite their elegant serenity, would

hardly have had such a universal success, if it had not been for the book in which he published them and his theory of architecture. Palladio's *Architettura* superseded Serlio's, especially after its revival in England early in the 18th century. His style appealed to the civilised taste and the polite learning of the Georgian gentry more than that of any other architect. Palladio is never dry or demonstratively

Fig. 33.—Andrea Palladio: Villa Trissino at Meledo.

scholarly. He combines the gravity of Rome with the sunny breadth of Northern Italy and an entirely personal ease not achieved by any of his contemporaries. In his Palazzo Chiericati (pl. XXVI A) of 1551–1557 the Tuscan Doric and correct Ionic order of the Bramante tradition with their straight entablatures are unmistakable. But the freedom in placing what had been confined to the courtyards of Roman palaces into the façade, thus opening up most of the façade and retaining only one solid piece in the centre of the first floor surrounded on all sides by air, is all Palladio's. He was especially fond of colonnades in his country houses, where he used them to connect a square main block with far reaching-out wings (fig. 33).

The contrast between solid and diffused had a great fascination for him. In one of his most complete schemes, the Villa Trissino at Meledo on the Venetian mainland (fig. 33), the house is almost completely symmetrical. The most extreme case, still existent and well preserved, of such extreme symmetry is the Villa Capra or Rotonda just outside Vicenza (pl. xxvi B, begun *c.* 1567), an academic achievement of high perfection and one specially admired by Pope's England. As a house to live in it has nothing of the informal snugness of the Northern manor house, but it has nobility and, with its slender Ionic porticoes, its pediments, its carefully placed few pedimented windows and its central dome, it appears stately without being pompous. Now to get the totality of a Palladian countryside composition one has to add to such a nucleus the curved colonnades and low outbuildings by which the villa takes in the land around. This embracing attitude proved of the greatest historical consequence. For here for the first time in Western architecture landscape and building were conceived as belonging to each other, as dependent on each other. Here for the first time the chief axes of a house are continued into nature; or alternatively the spectator standing outside sees the house spread out like a picture closing his vista. It is worth mentioning that in Rome at about the same time Michelangelo planned a comparable vista for the Palazzo Farnese which he had been commissioned to finish, across the Tiber with the Farnese gardens on the other side of the river.

It may seem odd to us that the Farnese family should have gone to Michelangelo the sculptor to complete their palace after San Gallo's death. But it must be remembered that Giotto was a painter and Brunelleschi a goldsmith. All the same, the story of how Michelangelo became an architect is worth telling, because it is equally characteristic of him and his age. He had as a boy been apprenticed to a painter, until, when Lorenzo the Magnificent had discovered him, given him lodgings in his palace and drawn him into his private circle, he was sent to learn in a freer, less mediæval way the art of sculpture from Lorenzo's favourite sculptor. His fame rested on sculpture. His huge David, the symbol of the civic pride of Renaissance Florence, he began at the age of twenty-six. A few years later Julius II commissioned him to prepare plans for an enormous tomb which the Pope wanted to erect for himself during his life-time. Michelangelo regarded it as his *magnum opus*. The first scheme provided for more than forty life-size or over life-size figures. The famous Moses is one of them. Architecture of course was also involved, though only as an accompaniment. However, when Julius had decided to rebuild St. Peter's to Bramante's design, he lost interest in the tomb and forced upon Michelangelo the task of painting the ceiling of the Sistine Chapel instead. Michelangelo never forgave Bramante for having, as he suspected, caused this change of mind. So for nearly five years—as he worked without an assistant—he had to stick to painting.

Then he returned to the tomb of Pope Julius, and perhaps in connection with conceptions that had passed through his mind when thinking of how architecturally to relate large figures with the wall against which they were going to stand, he began to take an interest in the plans of the Medici family to complete their church of S. Lorenzo in Florence by at last adding a façade. The church was Brunelleschi's work. Michelangelo in 1516 designed a façade two storeys high, with two orders and ample accommodation for sculpture. The commission was given to him, and for several years he worked in the quarries—a work he loved. Then however, in 1520, the Medicis found too many difficulties in the transport of the marble and cancelled the contract. But they made at once another one with Michelangelo for the erection of a family chapel or mausoleum by S. Lorenzo. This was in fact begun in 1521 and completed, though less ambitiously than originally planned, in 1534. The Medici Chapel is thus Michelangelo's first architectural work, and the work, it must be added, of one never initiated into the secrets of building technique and architectural drawing. It has already—though again chiefly conceived as background for sculpture—all the characteristics of his personal style. Architecture without any support from sculpture is to be found in his work for the first time in another job for the Medicis at S. Lorenzo, the library and the anteroom to the library (pl. XXVIII A). The library was designed in 1524, the anteroom (with the exception of the staircase for which the model was supplied as late as 1557) in 1526.

The anteroom is high and narrow. This alone gives an uncomfortable feeling. Michelangelo wanted to emphasise the contrast to the long, comparatively low and more restful library itself. The walls are divided into panels by coupled columns. At the ground floor height of the library itself the panels have blank windows and framed blank niches above. The colour scheme of the room is austere, a dead white against the sombre dark grey of columns, window niches, architraves and other structural or decorative members. As for the chief structural members, the columns, one would expect them to project and carry the architraves, as had always been the function of columns. Michelangelo reversed the relations. He recessed his columns and projected his panels so that they painfully encase the columns. Even the architraves go forward over the panels and backward over the columns. This seems arbitrary, just like the relations between ground-floor loggia and flat façade above or between second- and third-floor windows, in the Palazzo Massimi. It is certainly illogical, because it makes the carrying strength of the columns appear wasted. Moreover they have slender corbels at their feet which do not look substantial enough to support them and in fact do not support them at all. The thinness of the Massimi front characterises the blank windows with their tapering pilasters, fluted without any intelligible reason in one part only. The pediment over the entrance to the library is held only by the thin line around the door, raised into two square ears. The staircase tells of the same wilful originality; but the sharpness of detail which Michelangelo developed in the twenties is now replaced by a heavy, weary flow as of lava.

It has often been said that the motifs of the walls show Michelangelo as the father of the Baroque, because they express the superhuman struggle of active forces against overpowering matter. I do not think that anybody who examines without prejudice his sensations in the room itself would subscribe to this statement. There seems to me no expression of struggle anywhere, though there is conscious discordance all the way through. This austere animosity against the happy and harmonious we have seen already, although hidden under a polished formalism, in Giulio Romano. What Michelangelo's Laurenziana reveals is indeed Mannerism in its most sublime architectural form and not Baroque—a world of frustration much more tragic than the Baroque world of struggles between mind and matter. In Michelangelo's architecture every force seems paralysed. The load does not weigh, the support does not carry, natural reactions play no part—a highly artificial system upheld by the severest discipline.*

How remote does the warmth of the Renaissance seem amid these walls of frozen beauty. But then, was Michelangelo ever really of the Renaissance? In his Pietà of 1499 —yes. In his David—perhaps. In the Sistine Ceiling only to a limited extent; and after 1515 hardly ever. His character made it impossible for him to accept the ideals of the Renaissance for more than a short period. He was the very opposite of Castiglione's *Courtier* and Leonardo da Vinci: unsociable, distrustful, a fanatical worker, negligent in his personal appearance, deeply religious and uncompromisingly proud. Hence his dislike for Leonardo, and for Bramante and Raphael, a dislike made up of contempt and envy. We know more of his character and his life than in the case of any artist before. The unprecedented adoration for him caused the publication of two biographies while he was still alive, and biographies based on a systematic collecting of material. It is good that it should be so; for we feel we

---

* But to Jacob Burckhardt, the Swiss historian of the 19th century and the discoverer of the Renaissance in the sense in which we understand the style still to-day, the anteroom of the Laurenziana is but " an incomprehensible joke of the great master " (*Geschichte der Renaissance in Italien*, 7th edition, 1924, p. 208 ; written in 1867).

must know much about him to understand his art. In the Middle Ages the personality of an architect could never to that degree have influenced his style. Brunelleschi, though clearer to us as a character than the architects of the Gothic cathedrals, is still surprisingly objective in his forms. Michelangelo was the first to turn architecture into an instrument of individual expression. The *terribilità* that frightened those who met him fills us with awe immediately we are faced with any work of his, a room, a drawing, a piece of sculpture or a sonnet.

For Michelangelo was a consummate poet too, one of the profoundest of his age; and in his poems he gives to posterity a reckoning of his struggles. The fiercest of them was that between a Platonic ideal of beauty and a fervent faith in Christ. It is in the most concentrated form the struggle between the age of the Renaissance in which he lived when he was young, and that of the Counter-Reformation and Mannerism that began when he was about fifty years old, just before the sack of Rome in 1527. Now new stricter religious orders were founded, the Capuchins, the Oratorians, and above all the Jesuits (1534). Now new saints arose, St. Ignatius Loyola, St. Teresa, St. Philip Neri, St. Charles Borromeo. In 1542 the Inquisition was reintroduced, in 1543 literary censorship. In 1555 the Emperor Charles V abdicated and retired to the silence of a Spanish monastery. A few years later his son, Philip II, began his bleak and enormous palace of the Escorial, more a monastery than a palace. Spanish etiquette stood for a discipline as rigid as that of the early Jesuits and the Papal court of the same decades. In Rome nothing seemed left of Renaissance gaiety. The Venetian ambassadors wrote home that even the Carnivals were cold and lean. Paul V, the strictest of the Popes, had meat on his table only twice a week.

Michelangelo too had always been exemplarily sober and self-denying. He trained himself to need little sleep, and used to sleep with his boots on. While at work he sometimes fed on dry bread eaten without putting his tools aside. He felt his duties to his genius more heavily than the light-hearted architects of the Renaissance—and he could therefore venture to reply to a critic who objected to his having represented Giuliano de Medici on his tomb beardless, though he wore a beard in life: " Who in a thousand years will care for what he looked like ? " a saying utterly impossible before the Renaissance had freed the artist. For while the Middle Ages did not care for portrait likeness, because it is part of what is merely accidental in human nature, and while the early Renaissance had enjoyed portrait likeness, because it had only just discovered the artistic means for attaining it, Michelangelo refused to comply with it, because it would have hemmed in his æsthetic freedom. Yet his religious experience was of the most exacting, and it grew more so as he grew older and the century grew older, until he, the greatest sculptor of the West, and the most admired artist of his age, gave up painting and sculpture almost entirely. Architecture alone he still carried on, and he did not accept a salary for his work at St. Peter's.

The final break seems to have come after he had passed his seventieth year. Between the Medici Buildings of the mid-twenties and 1547 he seems to have designed and built only the fortifications of Florence in 1529—an engineering job, we would say, but a type of job in which Leonardo da Vinci and San Gallo, his predecessor in most of his Roman works, also excelled. In 1534 he had left Florence for good and gone to Rome. In 1535 Paul III appointed him Superintendent of the Vatican Buildings, an all but nominal appointment at first. In 1537 he was consulted about a more stately rebuilding of the municipal palaces on the Capitol; but nothing materialised. Then in 1546 San Gallo died, and now Michelangelo was called upon almost at once to complete the Palazzo Farnese, re-design St. Peter's, and re-plan the Capitol. At the Palazzo Farnese we shall now easily discover his Mannerism in the second-floor details (pl. xxvɪɪɪ B). The triplicating of the pilasters and especially the odd discordant framing of the windows with corbels on the sides not supporting anything and special corbels immediately above, on which the segmental pediments rest, are Michelangelo's personal expression, individual to an unprecedented extent and impossible before the breaking up first of the transcendentally ordered world of the Middle Ages and then of the æsthetically ordered world of the Renaissance.

Michelangelo's architectural masterpiece, the east parts and the dome of St. Peter's, are also an expression of revolt against Bramante and the spirit of the Renaissance, al-

Fig. 34.—Michelangelo Buonarroti: Plan for the completion of St. Peter's in Rome, 1546. Width *c.* 475 ft.

though they are not to the same extent Mannerist. When Michelangelo was appointed by Paul III, the Farnese Pope, to be architect of St. Peter's, he found the church essentially left as it had been at Bramante's death. Raphael and San Gallo had designed naves to comply with the religious demands of the first post-Renaissance generation. But they were not begun. Michelangelo returned to the central plan, but he deprived it of its all-governing balance (fig. 34). He kept the arms of the Greek cross, but where Bramante (fig. 31) had intended sub-centres repeating on a smaller scale the motif of the main centre, Michelangelo cut off the arms of the sub-centres, thus condensing the composition into one central dome resting on piers of a dimension that Bramante would have refused as colossal, i.e., inhuman, and a square ambulatory round. As for the exterior, he altered Bramante's plans in exactly the same spirit, replacing a happily balanced variety of noble and serene motifs by a huge order of Corinthian pilasters supporting a massive attic and by strangely incongruous windows and niches surrounded by *ædiculæ* and smaller niches of several sizes—a mighty yet somewhat discordant *ensemble*. At the West end, Michelangelo wanted to add a portico of ten columns with four columns in front of the middle ones. This—it was never built, because Maderna after 1600 added a nave—would have destroyed Bramante's ideal symmetry, and in fact the classic ideal of symmetry altogether; for the duplication of the centre columns is of course an utterly un-antique conception. Bramante's cupola was to be a perfect semi-sphere, Michelangelo's (pl. XXVII)—if we can take it that its present shape is Michelangelo's and not della Porta's who completed it in 1588–1590—is elongated and with the projecting coupled columns of the drum, the ribs up the dome and the coupled columns and concave top of the lantern a revision in very personal Renaissance forms of the essentially Gothic design of Brunelleschi's Florentine dome. Now the triumphant soar of this dome is not Mannerist. This superhuman victory of gigantic forces against huge masses points towards the Baroque. To admit that does not mean invalidating the thesis that Mannerism was the predominant tendency of later 16th-century architecture. It merely means admitting the vastness of Michelangelo's genius. He—and the same is true of the other greatest masters of his generation, of Raphael and Titian—in growing out of, and beyond, the Renaissance conceived both the styles of the 16th and the 17th centuries. The 16th followed his manner and turned it into Mannerism, the 17th appre ciated the *terribilità* of his conflicts and made Baroque out of it. So the eternal city is crowned not by a symbol of Renaissance worldliness, as Julius II had visualised it, but by an overwhelming synthesis of Mannerism and Baroque, and at the same time of Antiquity and Christianity.

It was Michelangelo's last three-dimensional work of such violence. He was seventy-two when he designed it. The eighteen years that were left to him he spent in meditation on life after death. " Let there be no more painting, no more carving," he says in one of his late sonnets, " to soothe the soul turned towards that Divine Love which opened His arms from the cross to receive us."

> " Nè pinger ne scolpir fia più che quieti
> L'anima volta a quell' Amor Divino
> C'aperse, a prender noi, 'n croce le Braccia."

He carved after this only three more groups, all three Entombments of Christ. One of them was for his own tomb, one he left unfinished, or rather sublimated to so immaterial a form that it can no longer be regarded as sculpture in the Renaissance sense. His late drawings too are spiritualised to a degree almost unbearable in an artist who had done more than any before him to glorify the beauty and vigour of body and movement. And one of his last architectural plans—a fact not widely enough known—was to design the Roman church of the newly founded, severely counter-reformatory order of the Jesuits. He offered to take charge of the building without any fee, just as he had refused to accept a salary as architect to St. Peter's.

The Gesù was not begun until four years after Michelangelo's death. It has perhaps exerted a wider influence than any other church of the last four hundred years (fig. 35). Giacomo Vignola (1507–73) the architect, following probably Michelangelo's ideas, combines in his ground plan the central scheme of the Renaissance with the longitudinal scheme of the Middle Ages—an eminently characteristic fact. The combination as such is not new. Alberti had done the same a hundred years before at S. Andrea in Mantua (fig. 28). The façade too (fig. 36) seems to take up a theme that Alberti had conceived. The problem for architects of the Renaissance, and since the Renaissance, was how to project the dimensions of tall nave and lower aisles on to the exterior without abandoning the orders of classical architecture. Alberti's solution was to have a ground floor on the triumphal arch system and a top floor the width of the nave only but with volutes, i.e., scrolls, rising towards it from the entablature in front of the lean-to roofs of the aisles. This method was adopted by Vignola in his design for the Gesù façade (though with the

Fig. 35.—Giacomo Vignola: Church of Jesus (Gesù), Rome, begun 1568. Length inside *c.* 225 ft.

fuller and less harmonious orchestration of his age), and then by della Porta who substituted a new design for Vignola's. It has been repeated innumerable times and with many variations in the Baroque churches of Italy and the other Roman Catholic countries.

As for the interior (pl. XXIX A) Vignola keeps Alberti's interpretation of the aisles as series of chapels opening into the nave. He does not however concede them as much independence as the Renaissance architect considered necessary, always anxious as he was to let every part of a building be a whole. The extreme width of the nave under its powerful barrel-vault degrades the chapels into mere

niches accompanying a vast hall, and it has been suggested
(Weise) that this motif was chosen by the Jesuits themselves
to whom it was familiar from the Late Gothic churches of
Spain with their chapels between the buttresses and some-

Fig. 36.—Giacomo Vignola's design for the front of the Gesù.

times a passage connecting them (see page 73). If the suggestion is accepted, there is here yet another instance of the post-Renaissance return to mediæval ideals—another, after the revival of Catholic faith which showed itself in the new Saints and the new Orders, after the Gothic curve of the dome of St. Peter's and the re-introduction of a longitudinal emphasis in the Gesù plan. In the Gesù this emphasis on the eastward drive is obviously deliberate. The barrel-vault and above all the main cornice, running all the way through without a break, take it up most eloquently in the elevation. There is however one element in Vignola's design that it would be impossible to find in the same sense in any mediæval church: the light. In the cathedral of the 13th century the stained-glass windows glow by means of light penetrating, but light itself is not a positive value. Later on in the Decorated style, light begins to model walls with their ogee-arched niches and play over filigree decoration, but it is never a major factor of architectural design. In the Gesù on the other hand certain important features are introduced into the composition exclusively in order to make light-effects possible. The nave is lit from windows above the chapels—an even, subdued light. Then the last bay before the dome is shorter, less open and darker than the others. This contraction in space and lightness prepares dramatically for the majestic crossing with its mighty cupola. The floods of light streaming down from the windows of the drum create that sensation of fulfilment that Gothic architects achieved in so much less sensuous a way.

The decoration of the Gesù appears sensuous too, luxurious though sombre. However, it is not of Vignola's day. He would have been more moderate, with smaller motifs and a shallower relief; this is certain from what we know of late 16th-century decoration. Thus the effect of the mediæval movement towards the East would have been much stronger, with less to deflect attention from the cornice and the mighty barrel-vault. The re-decoration was done in 1668–83. It belongs to the High Baroque, whereas the building is, to say it again, Mannerist, neither of the equanimity of all High Renaissance, nor of the expansive vigour of all Baroque.

A. Baldassare Peruzzi: Palazzo Massimi, Rome, begun 1535. B. Giulio
Romano: house, Mantua, c. 1544.

Andrea Palladio: *A.* Palazzo Chierigati, Vicenza, 1551–57. *B.* Vi
Rotonda near Vicenza, begun *c.* 1567.

Michelangelo: the dome of St. Peter's, Rome, designed 1558–60, completed by Giacomo della Porta 1588–90.

A. Michelangelo: Laurenziana Library, Florence, ante-room, designed 1526, staircase 1557.   B. Antonio da San Gallo: Palazzo Farnese, Rome, 1530–46.   The top storey by Michelangelo.

A. Giacomo Vignola: Church of the Gesù, Rome, begun 1568. B. Francesco Borromini: S. Carlo alle Quattro Fontane, Rome, begun 1633.

XXIX

A. Francesco Borromini : S. Carlo alle Quattro Fontane, Rome, façade 1667. *B.* Gian Lorenzo Bernini : Altar of St. Theresa, S. Maria della Vittoria, Rome, 1646.

XXXI

A. Gian Lorenzo Bernini : Royal Staircase (Scala Regia), Vatican Palace, Rome, *c.* 1660–70. *B.* Narciso Tomé: Trasparente, Cathedral, Toledo : completed 1732.

B Cosmas Damian and Egid ... (Sparia) Granada 1727-64

CHAPTER SIX

THE BAROQUE IN THE ROMAN CATHOLIC COUNTRIES
(*c.* 1600–*c.* 1760)

MANNERISM, it has been pointed out, was originally, and in this country still is, a noun connected with " mannered " and nothing else. In Continental and American terminology however, some twenty years ago, it changed its meaning and became the term for a specific historic style in art, the post-Renaissance style of the 16th century, particularly in Italy. The same process had taken place about fifty years earlier with regard to Baroque. Baroque had originally signified odd, especially of odd shape. It was therefore adopted to describe an architectural style which to the classicist appeared to revel in odd, extravagant shapes, that is the style of the 17th century. Then, chiefly in the 'eighties of the last century and chiefly in Germany, it lost its derogatory flavour and became a neutral term to designate the works of art of that century. It is now fairly familiar as such in Britain too.*

We have seen the Baroque style first heralded in the massive forms and the gigantic *excelsior* of the dome of Michelangelo's St. Peter's. We have then seen that these efforts of Michelangelo towards the Baroque remained exceptional and that he himself in other works of architecture gave way to the pressure of Mannerism. It was only after Mannerism had completed its course that a new generation at the beginning of the 17th century, especially in Rome, tired of the forced austerity of the late 16th, rediscovered Michelangelo as the father of the Baroque. The style thus introduced culminated in Rome between 1630 and

---

* But as late as 1927 it was printed in an accepted English text-book of the history of architecture that Baroque signifies "a heavy and clumsy treatment of Renaissance architecture, with coarse and florid detail.", and that it is " improperly used to denote a supposed 'style' which has no existence as the style of any period ".

1670, and then left Rome, first for the North of Italy (Guarini and Juvara in Piedmont) and then for Spain and Portugal and Germany and Austria. Rome, since the late 17th century, turned back to its classical tradition, partly under the influence of Paris. For the Paris of Richelieu, Colbert and Louis XIV had become the centre of European art, a position which until then Rome had held unchallenged for well over 150 years.

The Popes and cardinals of the 17th century were enthusiastic patrons, eager to commemorate their names by magnificent churches, palaces and tombs. Of the severity of fifty years ago, when the Counter-Reformation had been a militant force, nothing was left. The Jesuits became more and more lenient, the most popular saints were of a lovable, gentle, accommodating kind (such as St. François de Sales), and the new experimental science was promoted under the very eyes of the popes, until in the 18th century Benedict XIV could accept books which Voltaire and Montesquieu sent him as presents.

However, a general decline in the religious fervour of the people can hardly be noticed before 1660 or even later. Not the intensity of religious feelings, only their nature changed. Art and architecture prove that unmistakably. We can here analyse but a few examples, and it is therefore advisable not to choose the most magnificent, say the nave and façade of St. Peter's, as Carlo Maderna designed them in 1606, and as they were completed in 1626, but the most concentrated.

Maderna was the leading architect of his generation in Rome. He died in 1629. His successors in fame were Gianlorenzo Bernini (1598–1667) and Francesco Borromini (1599–1667). Bernini came from Naples, Maderna and Borromini from the North of Italy, the country round the lakes. As in the 16th century, so there were in the 17th only very few Romans amongst the great men of Rome. In architecture the influx from Lombardy had a considerable effect on the appearance of the city. A breadth and freedom were introduced in distinct contrast to Roman gravity. Thus Maderna's ground plan of the Palazzo Barberini (fig. 37)—its façade is by Bernini and a good deal of its decorative detail by Borromini—is of a kind wholly new in Rome. As against the austere blocks of the Florentine and Roman palaces (cf. the Palazzo Farnese, fig. 32), the Barberini Palace has a front opened in a wide loggia and with short wings jutting forward on the right and the left. The Roman plan with colonnaded inner courtyard is, one might say, cut into two, and only one half remains. The colonnades are now part of the façade. This exposing to the public of what had until then been kept private is eminently

Fig. 37.—Carlo Maderna (and Gianlorenzo Bernini?): Palazzo Barberini, Rome, begun 1628.

characteristic of the Baroque, as will be seen presently. The main staircase of the Barberini Palace also is wider and more open than those of the 16th century, and the semi-circular room in the centre, as well as the oval saloon to which it leads, are forms that the architect might have found in Roman churches and in the ruins of Imperial Rome, but that in domestic architecture seem distinctly in the spirit of Palladio (and the Lombards too).

It is important to remember that when Bernini with his

South-Italian impetuosity won the first place in Roman sculpture and architecture, this infiltration of North Italian elegance had already done its work. His noble colonnades in front of St. Peter's have something of the happy openness of Palladian villa architecture, in spite of their Roman weight and their Berninesque sculptural vigour. For Bernini was the son of a sculptor and himself the greatest sculptor of the Baroque. He incidentally, also painted, and as for his reputation as an architect, it was so great that Louis XIV invited him to Paris to design plans for an enlargement of the Louvre Palace. Bernini was as universal as Michelangelo, and nearly as famous. Borromini on the other hand was trained as a mason, and, since he was distantly related to Maderna, found work in a small way at St. Peter's, when he went to Rome at the age of fifteen. There he worked on, humble and unknown, while Bernini created his first masterpiece of Baroque decoration, the bronze canopy under Michelangelo's dome, in the centre of St. Peter's, a huge monument, nearly 100 feet high, and with its four gigantic twisted columns the very symbol of the changed age, of a grandeur without restraint, a wild extravagance, and a luxury of detail that would have been distasteful to Michelangelo.

The same vehemence of approach and the same revolutionary disregard of conventions characterise Borromini's first important work, the church of S. Carlo alle Quattro Fontane (pl. XXIX B), begun in 1633. The interior is so small that it would fit into one of the piers which support the dome of St. Peter's. But in spite of its miniature size it is one of the most ingenious spatial compositions of the century. It has been said before that the normal plan for longitudinal churches of the Baroque was that of the Gesù: nave with side chapels, short transepts, and dome over the crossing. But the centralised ground plan was not given up either. It was only the predominance of the circle in central churches which the Baroque discarded in Rome. Instead of the circle the oval was introduced (already in Vignola's S. Anna dei Palafrenieri), a less finite form, and a form that endows the centralised plan with longitudinal elements i.e., elements suggestive of movement in space. In S. Carlo the oval is placed into a West–East direction, in other churches (e.g., Bernini's S. Andrea al Quirinale) it lies across from South to North. Both systems spread, inside and outside Italy.

Spatial clarity had been the ideal of Renaissance planning. Each feature was kept clear of the next. The eye of the spectator had to be able to run unimpeded from one to another and read the meaning of the whole and the parts

Fig. 38.—Francesco Borromini: S. Carlo alle Quattro Fontane, begun 1633. Front, 1667.

without effort. Now all this is reversed. Nobody, standing in S. Carlo, can at once understand of what elements it is made, and how they are intertwined to produce such a rolling, rocking effect. To analyse the ground plan (fig. 38) it will be best to set out from the domed Greek cross of the Renaissance. Borromini has given the dome absolute supremacy over the arms. Their corners are bevelled off so that the walls under the oval dome read like an elongated lozenge opening out into shallow chapels, the dwarfed arms of the original Greek cross. The chapels on the right and

the left are fragments of ovals again.   If drawn out, they
would meet in the centre of the building.   The entrance
chapel and the apsidal chapel are also fragments of ovals.
They just touch the side ovals.   Thus five compound
spatial shapes merge into each other.   We can stand nowhere without taking part in the swaying rhythm of several
of them.   The Late Gothic churches of Germany had
achieved a similar wealth of spatial relations, but by means
of forms that seem wiry when compared with the undulating
walls of S. Carlo.·   Michelangelo is responsible for this turn
of architecture towards the plastic.   Space now seems
hollowed out by the hand of a sculptor, walls are moulded as if
made of wax or clay.

Borromini's most daring enterprise in setting whole walls
into motion is the façade of S. Carlo which was added in
1667, the year of his death (pl. xxx A).   The ground floor
and its cornice give the main theme: concave—convex—
concave.   But the first floor answers by a concave-concave-
concave flow, complicated by the insertion of a kind of
flattened-out miniature oval temple set into the centre con-
cavity so that this bay seems convex as long as one does
not look up to its top part.   Such relations in volume and
space sound dry when described; when seen, however, there
is *brio* and passion in them, and also something distinctly
voluptuous.   Never before had architecture so much played
up to physical sensations.   No doubt Borromini knew that
he was going to shock—that is a new attitude in the artist
too.   His detail is deliberately novel, from the curious oval
windows on the ground floor with palm leaves around, a
crown above, and some sort of a Roman altar in relief
beneath, to the ogee arch crowning the façade, and the poly-
gons of odd shapes and diminishing sizes that decorate the
cupola inside.   But Baroque details are senseless, unless
they are seen as parts of a super-ordinate decorative whole.

To understand the Baroque it is essential to see it in this
perspective.   We are too much used—especially in this
country—to looking at decoration as something that may
or may not be added to architecture.   In fact all architecture is both structure and decoration, decoration for which
the architect himself, or the sculptor, the painter, the glass-

painter may be responsible. But the relation of decoration to structure varies in different ages and with different nations. In the Gothic style of the cathedrals all decoration served the mason's work. Then ornamental sculpture, late in the 13th and early in the 14th century, seemed to overgrow structure. Then, again somewhat later, figure sculpture and painting freed themselves from the supremacy of architecture altogether. A monument like Verrocchio's Colleoni in Venice, standing free in a square without any architectural support, would have been inadmissible in the Middle Ages. Just as novel was the conception of easel painting as such, painting independent of the wall against which it was going to be placed. The Renaissance accepted the independence of the fine arts, but was able to hold them together within a building, because of the principle of relatively independent parts that governed all Renaissance composition. Now however, in the Baroque, that principle had been abandoned. Again, as in Gothic architecture, parts cannot be isolated. We have seen that at S. Carlo. But the Baroque, although believing in the unity of all art, could not restore the supremacy of structure. Architects of the 17th century had to accept the claims of the sculptor and painter, and in fact often were sculptors and painters. Instead of the Gothic relation of superordinate and subordinate, there is now a co-operation of all the arts. The result was still that " *Gesamtkunstwerk* " (total art) which Wagner, in his operas, after it had been wilfully destroyed at the end of the Baroque, endeavoured in vain to recover for the 19th century. In the works of Bernini and Borromini, what binds architectural, ornamental, sculptural and pictorial effects into indivisible unity is the decorative principle common to all.

Now this decorative creed could leave no room in the minds of patrons and artists of the Baroque to be squeamish about honesty in the use of materials. As long as the effect was attained, what could it matter whether you attained it with marble or with stucco, with gold or with tin, with a real bridge or a sham bridge such as we find sometimes in English parks? Optical illusion is in fact (to Ruskin's grave displeasure) amongst the most characteristic devices of Baroque architecture. Bernini's Royal Staircase, the *Scala Regia* in the Vatican Palace (pl. XXXI A and fig. 39), illustrates this at its most suggestive. It was built during the same sixties which saw Borromini's façade of S. Carlo rise from the ground and Bernini's oval colonnades in front of St. Peter's. As they are a masterpiece of stage setting, seemingly raising the height and weight of Maderna's façade, and at the same time

Fig. 39.—Gianlorenzo Bernini: The Royal Staircase (Scala Regia) in the Vatican Palace, Rome, *c.* 1665.

making the loggia of the Papal benedictions and the *Porta Santa* visible to everybody amongst the tens of thousands who would stand in the forecourt on the occasion of great celebrations, so is the Scala Regia designed with a supreme knowledge of scenic effects. It is the main entrance to the palace. Coming from the colonnades, one reaches it along a corridor. The corridor ends in about fifteen or twenty steps, and then there is a slight break just at the point where one enters at right angles from the galilee porch of St. Peter's. So here two main directions meet. They had to be joined and connected up. It was a master-stroke of Bernini to place opposite the entrance from the Church an equestrian monument to the Emperor Constantine. Coming up from the corridor it appears on the right and forces us to halt, before we enter the Royal Staircase itself. The sudden appearance of the white prancing horse against a storm-swept drapery lit by windows above serves to conceal the otherwise unpleasant change of direction.

The *Scala Regia* had to be fitted into an awkwardly shaped area between church and palace. It is long, comparatively narrow and has irregularly converging walls. Bernini turned all this to advantage by means of an ingenious barrel-vaulted colonnade of diminishing size. The principle is that of vistas on the Baroque stage. Streets there were made to appear long by the use of exaggerated perspective. In the same way Borromini treated the niches at S. Carlo (pl. xxix B) and the windows on the top floor of the Palazzo Barberini. Such scenic illusions were not entirely new. They are to be found in Bramante's early works in Milan. Michelangelo too in his design for the Capitol in Rome had placed the palaces on the sides at such an angle as to increase the apparent width of the square. Light is another means for dramatising the ascent up the Royal Staircase. On the first landing halfway up it falls in from the left, on the second in the far distance a window faces the staircase and dissolves the contours of the room. Finally there is the decoration, the splendid angels, e.g., with their trumpets holding up the Pope's arms, to complete this gorgeous overture to the Vatican palace.

Angels, genii and such-like figures, preferably in realistic colouring, are an essential part of Baroque settings. Not only do they serve to cover up structural joints and to hide the contraptions " behind the scenes " which make these illusions work, but they also act as intermediaries between the real space in which we move and the space created by the artist. The Baroque does not want to keep the border line visible between audience and stage. Such terms from the world of the theatre—or should one rather say : the world of the opera which was an Italian invention of the 17th century—come into one's mind with good reason. However, there is more than a mere theatrical trick in this flow from reality into illusion and from illusion into reality. Bernini's famous chapel of St. Teresa in the church of S. Maria della Vittoria in Rome proves that (pl. xxx B). The chapel, which dates from 1646, is faced with dark marbles, their gleaming surfaces of amber, gold and pink reflecting the light in ever-changing patterns. In the middle of the wall in front of the entrance is the altar of the Saint. It is flanked by heavy coupled columns and pilasters with a broken pediment, placed on the slant so that they come forward towards us and then recede to focus our attention on the centre of the altar, where one would expect to find a painting, but where there is a niche with a sculptural group, treated like a picture and giving an illusion of reality that is as startling to-day as it was three hundred years ago. Everything in the chapel contributes to this *peinture vivante* illusion. Along the walls on the right and the left there are also niches opened into the chapel walls, and there Bernini has portrayed in marble, behind balconies, members of the Cornaro family, the donors of the chapel, watching with us the miraculous scene, precisely as though they were in the boxes, and we in the stalls of a theatre.

The boundary line between our world and the world of art is in this most ingeniously effaced. As our own attention and that of the marble figures is directed towards the same goal, we cannot help giving the same degree of reality first to them as to ourselves, and then to the figures on the altar too. And Bernini has used all his mastery in the modelling of St. Teresa and the angel to help in that deception. The heavy cloak of the nun, the fluffiness of the clouds, the light drapery of the youthful angel and his soft flesh are all rendered with an exquisite realism. The expression of the Saint in the miracle of the union with Christ is of an unforgettable voluptuous ecstasy. She faints as though overwhelmed by a physical penetration. At the same time she is raised into the air, and the diagonal sweep of the group makes us believe the impossible. Beams of gold—they are gilt metal shafts—conceal the back wall of

the niche, and an opening high up behind the entablature
glazed with a yellow pane models the scene with a magical
light.

The Chapel of St. Teresa is the most daring example of
such illusionism in Rome. It is in fact an exception.
Rome has never really believed in extremes. Bernini was a
Neapolitan; and Naples was Spanish. To experience the
thrills of extremes and excesses one must indeed go to
Spain, or else to Portugal, or of course Germany. To
these countries the Baroque came late, but it was taken up
with tremendous fervour. Italy has no examples of such
orgiastic interpenetration of reality and fiction as can be
seen in some few Spanish and many more South German
churches of the early 18th century.

The most outstanding example on Spanish soil is Narciso
Tomé's *Trasparente* in Toledo Cathedral (pl. xxxi B). The
cathedral is a 13th-century building in the style of classic
French Gothic. It has a high altar with a vast Late Gothic
reredos. Catholic orthodoxy objected to people walking
along the ambulatory behind the Blessed Sacrament. So
an ingenious plan was worked out by which the Sacrament
could be seen and would be respected from the ambulatory
as well. It was placed in a glass-fronted receptacle—hence
the name *Trasparente*—and an altar scenery was built up
around it of unheard-of pomp. The work was completed
in 1732. Attention was focused on to the Sacrament
by richly decorated columns. They are linked up with
large outer columns by cornices curved upwards. These
curves and the relief scenes in perspective on the panels
below give the illusion—in the same way as Bernini's
colonnade in the *Scala Regia*—as though the distance from
front to back of the altar were far deeper than it really is.
Moreover, the glass-fronted opening is surrounded by angels
to cover all structural props. By the clouds of angels our
eyes are led up to where the Last Supper is acted—at a
fantastic height—by figures of polychromatic marble.
Higher up still is the Virgin soaring up to Heaven. To
enhance the effect of a miraculous apparition, the whole
scene is floodlit from behind where we stand while we
stare at it, lit that is in the way special stage lighting is

Fig. 40.—Narciso Tomé: Trasparente in the cathedral of Toledo, completed 1732.

operated to-day. What the ingenious architect has done is to take out the masonry between the ribs of half a Gothic vault of the ambulatory—the engineering genius of the 13th century allowed him to do so without weakening the construction—spread groups of angels around the opening, and then erect above it a dormer with a window, invisible from below, which lets in a flood of golden light past the angels and the bay of the ambulatory in which we stand, on to the altar with its figures and the Sacrament. And when, to discover this source of magic light, we turn round, away from the altar, we see in the dazzling light beyond the angels Christ himself seated on clouds, and prophets and the Heavenly Host surrounding him.

Such spatial extremism, the pulling of a whole room into one vast stupefying ornament, is, it has been said before, exceptional in Spain. What Spain and Portugal excelled in was this same extremism expressing itself in the piling of ornament on to surfaces. This ornamental mania had been a Spanish heritage ever since Mohammedan times, the Alhambra, and the Late Gothic of such works as the front of St. Paul's at Valladolid (pl. xx B), but never yet had it taken quite such fantastic shapes as it now did in the so-called Churrigueresque style, named after its chief exponent José de Churriguera (1650–1725). The immediate inspiration of the barbaric scrolls and thick mouldings of, e.g., the Sacristy of the Charterhouse at Granada (1727–64; pl. XXXII A; by F. Manuel Vasquez) must have been native art of Central or South America, as the immediate inspiration of the Manueline style in Portugal has been found in the East Indies. It is in fact in Mexico that the Spanish architects celebrated the wildest of all orgies of over-decoration.

The *Trasparente* stands on a higher æsthetic level no doubt than the incrustations of the Churrigueresque, though morally, especially to the Ruskinian morality of Late Victorian England, they may both be equally objectionable. Southern Germany in the 18th century was almost as fond of ornament for ornament's sake as Spain. There again the tradition leads back to the Middle Ages. But as it has been shown that German Late Gothic was fonder of spatial complexity than the Late Gothic of any other country, so the exploitation of space became now the central problem of German Late Baroque, a problem occasionally solved with the knock-out technique of the *Trasparente*, but more often by purer strictly architectural means.

Two architects only out of the many working between 1720 and 1760 can here be introduced: Cosmas Damian Asam (1686–1739) and Johann Balthasar Neumann (1687–1753).

Cosmas Damian Asam was a painter and decorator, his brother Egid Quirin (1692–1750) a sculptor. The two as a rule worked together, not considered as anything but competent craftsmen and not apparently considering themselves as anything else either. They, and in common with them the majority of the German 18th-century architects, were not really architects in the Renaissance or modern sense. They were brought up in villages to know something about building, and that was enough. No big ideas about professional status entered their heads. In fact the sociological position of architecture in Germany before the 19th century was still mediæval, and most of the patrons were still princes, bishops, abbots, just as they had been three hundred years earlier. Neumann belongs to another category, one that had not existed in the Middle Ages or the Renaissance. Its source is the France of Louis XIV, as will be shown later (see p. 173). He had started in the artillery force of the Prince-Bishop of Würzburg. There he had shown a keen interest in mathematics and fortification. Michelangelo too, it will be remembered, had worked on the defence engineering, and some of the other leading 16th-century architects in Italy, e.g., Sammicheli, had been distinguished military engineers. The Prince-Bishop singled out young Neumann for architectural work, made him his surveyor of works and sent him to Paris and Vienna to discuss the plans for his new palace at Würzburg with his opposite numbers there, the French King's and the Emperor's architects, and to learn from them. Thus his most famous work, the palace at Würzburg, is only partly his; but his experience grew, and the Bishop appreciated him more and more. He was made a Captain, then a Major, then a Colonel, but he had no longer any duties of active service and could devote all his time to architecture. He did all the designing and supervising for the Bishop that had to be done, and was soon also asked to design palaces and churches for other clients.

Thus churches of the 18th century in Germany may originate from very different *milieus*: the workshop of the mediæval craftsman or the drawing-board of the technically skilled courtier. Differences in architectural character may often be explained in this way. Asam churches are naïve, Neumann's are of an intellectual complexity equal to Bach's. Spatial effects, however, are as important in the Asams' as in Neumann's work. But the Asams stick to the more ostentatious devices of optical illusion (raising them, it is true, to a high emotional pitch), while Neumann composes his configurations of space scorning easy deceptions.

At Rohr near Ratisbon the Asams, instead of a High Altar, placed in the chancel of the church a show-piece, cruder than Bernini's St. Teresa, and twice as melodramatic: the Apostles, life-size figures standing around a life-size Baroque sarcophagus, and the Virgin rising to Heaven supported by angels to be received into a glory of clouds and cherubs high above. Wild gesticulation and dark glowing colour all help to inflame the passions of faith. The chancel at Weltenburg, another church near Ratisbon, is the stage for a more mysterious apparition: a silver St. George on horseback wielding a flame-shaped sword and riding straight towards us out of a background of dazzling light which is let in from concealed windows. The dragon and the princess stand out as dark golden silhouettes against all this glitter. Rohr was built in 1718–25, Weltenberg in 1717–21. They are early works of the Asams.

In their best later work they endeavoured to achieve more than a *Trasparente* effect. Egid Quirin owned a house at Munich; when he approached the age of forty he began to think of a monument that he might proudly leave behind after his death. So he decided in 1731 to build on a site adjoining his house a church as his private offering. The church was built from 1733 to about 1750 and dedicated to St. John Nepomuk. It is a tiny church (pl. XXXII B) less than thirty feet wide, relatively tall and narrow with a narrow gallery all the way round, a ground-floor altar and a gallery altar. The gallery balancing on the fingers of pirouetting termini or caryatid angels sways forward and backward, the top cornice surges up and droops down, the colour scheme is of sombre gold, browns and dark reds, glistening in sudden flashes where light falls on it, light which comes only from the entrance, that is from behind our backs, and from concealed windows above the cornice. The top East window is placed in such a way that a group of the Trinity appears against it; God holding the Crucifixus, and the Holy Ghost above, the whole again surrounded by angels—wildly fantastic, yet of a superb magic reality. What raises St. John Nepomuk above the level of Rohr, Weltenburg and the *Trasparente* is the co-operation of strictly architectural composition with the merely optical deceptions to achieve an intense sensation of surprise which may turn easily into religious fervour.

But sensational it is all the same, sensational in a literal sense: no artists before Bernini, the Asams and Tomé have aimed at such violent effects. And are they therefore debauched, unscrupulous, and pagan as our Pugins and Ruskins have made them out? We should not accept their verdicts uncritically, lest we might deprive ourselves of a good deal of legitimate pleasure. We may indeed, up here in the North, where we live, find it hard to connect Christ and the Church with this obtruding physical closeness of presentation. To the Southerner, in Bavaria, in Austria, in Italy, in Spain, where people live so much more with all their senses, it is a genuine form of religious experience. While in the North during the lifetime of Bernini, the Asams and Tomé, Spinoza visualised a pantheism, with God pervading all beings and all things, Rembrandt discovered the infinite for painting in his treatment of light and his merging of action into undefined but live background, and Newton and Leibniz discovered it for mathematics in their conception of the calculus, the South had its more concrete realisation of an all-embracing oneness and a presence of the infinite in the architects' and decorators' unification of real and fictitious worlds, and in their spatial effects stepping beyond the bounds of what the beholder can rationally explain to himself. And Neumann's work proves conclusively what architectural purity and subtlety can be achieved by such spatial magic, provided the visitor to his buildings is able to follow his guidance. We of the 20th century do not usually find it easy to concentrate on spatial counterpoint just as our audiences in church and concert no doubt hear musical counterpoint less distinctly than those for whom Bach wrote. The parallelism is in fact striking, in quality too. The best German 18th-century architecture is up to the standard of the best German 18th-century music.

Take Neumann's pilgrimage church of Vierzehnheiligen in Franconia, built from 1743 to 1772 (pl. xxxiv). The first impression on entering this vast, solitary pilgrimage church is one of bliss and elation. All is light: white, gold, pink. In this the church testifies to its later date than that of St. John Nepomuk. Asam's work is still Baroque in the 17th-century sense, Neumann's belongs to that last phase of the Baroque which goes under the name Rococo. For the Rococo is not a separate style. It is part of the Baroque, as Decorated is part of the Gothic style. The difference of Baroque and Rococo is only one of sublimation. The later phase is light, where the earlier was sombre; delicate, where the earlier was forceful; playful, where the earlier was passionate. But it is just as *mouvementé*, as vivacious, as voluptuous as the Baroque. One connects the term Rococo chiefly with France and the age of Casanova on the one hand, Voltaire on the other. In Germany it is not intellectually or sensually sophisticated—it is as direct an expression of the people's æsthetic instinct as late Gothic architecture and decoration had been, and one can see from the devotion to-day of the peasants in these German Baroque—and the Italian Baroque—churches that their style is not a style of interest only to a privileged set of virtuosi.

Yet the style of Vierzehnheiligen is not an easy style. It is not enough to be overwhelmed by it, as anyone may be in Asam churches; it asks for an exact understanding—which is a job for the expert: architects' architecture, as the fugue is musicians' music. The oval central altar in the middle of the nave may well please the rustic worshippers who kneel round this gorgeous object, half a coral reef and half a fairy sedan chair. Having taken in this glory of confectionery, the layman will then look up and see on all sides glittering decoration, surf and froth and rocket, and like it immensely. But if he starts walking round, he will soon find himself in utter confusion. What he has learned and so often seen of nave and aisle and chancel seems of no value here. This confusion of the lay mind, a keen thrill of the trained, is due to the ground plan, one of the most ingenious pieces of architectural design ever conceived (fig. 41). The church, if one looks at it from outside, has

Fig. 41.—Balthasar Neumann: Vierzehnheiligen near Bamberg, Franconia, begun 1743. Length *c.* 210 ft.

apparently a nave and aisles, and a centrally planned East end with polygonal ends to transepts and choir. In fact the choir is an oval, the transepts are circular, and the nave consists of two ovals following each other so that the first, into which one enters immediately one has passed the Borrominesque undulating front, is of the size of the choir oval and the second considerably larger. It is here that the altar of the fourteen saints stands. Here then is the spiritual centre of the church. So there arises an antagonism of great poignancy between what the exterior promises as the centre and what the interior reveals to be the centre—namely between the crossing where nave and transepts meet, and

he centre of the principal oval. As for the aisles they are
nothing but spatial residues. Walking along them, one
feels painfully behind the scenes. What matters alone is the
interaction of the ovals. At vault height they are separated
by transverse arches. These however are not simple bands
across from one arcade column to the one opposite. They
are three-dimensional, bowing to each other, as the nodding
arches had done on a small scale in the 14th century. This
has the most exciting and baffling effect at the crossing. Here
in a church of the Gesù type—and Vierzehnheiligen appears
from outside to belong to this type—one would expect a
dome, the summit of the composition. Instead of that,
there lies, as has been said before, just at the centre of the
crossing, the point where choir oval and central oval meet.
The two transverse arches struck from the piers of the
crossing bend, the Western one Eastward, the Eastern Westward until they touch each other in exactly the same place as
the ovals, purposely emphasising the fact that, where a normal Baroque church would have had the crest of the undulating movement of the vaults, Vierzehnheiligen has a
trough—a most effective spatial counterpoint. Yet another
spatial complication is incidentally provided by the insertion
of a second minor transept further West than the main one.
Side altars are placed in it, just as altars stand against the
East end of the church and against the East piers of the
crossing. The latter are set diagonally so as to guide the eye
towards the splendid high altar—a decidedly theatrical effect.

This is one of the chief objections against such churches.
Its validity has already been queried. Besides, why did architects and artists so fervently strive to deceive and create such
intense illusion of reality? What reality was the Church
concerned with? Surely that of the divine presence. It is the
zeal of an age in which Roman Catholic dogmas, mysteries
and miracles, were no longer, as they had been in the Middle
Ages, accepted as truth by all. There were heretics, and
there were sceptics. To restore the first to the fold, to con-
vince the others, religious architecture had both to inflame
and to mesmerise. But, it is brought forward as another
argument against Baroque churches, that they seem worldly
as compared with the churches of the Middle Ages. Now

it is true that the character of Baroque decoration in a church
and a palace is identical. But is not exactly the same true
of the Middle Ages? The idea behind the identity is perfectly
sane. By the splendour of the arts we honour a King; i.
not supreme splendour due to the King of Kings? In our
churches to-day and in those churches of the Middle Age
which the 19th century restored, there is nothing of this
They are halls with an atmosphere to concentrate the
thoughts of a congregation on worship and prayer. A
church of the Baroque was literally the house of the Lord.

Still, there is no denying the fact that we, observers o

Fig. 42.—Plan for the rebuilding of the monastery of Weingarten, 172.

believers, never feel quite sure where in a church such a
Vierzehnheiligen the spiritual ends and the worldly begin
The ecstatic *élan* of the architectural forms at large is irre
sistible, but it is not necessarily a religious *élan*. There wa
it is true, a real mania in Southern Germany and Austri
between 1700 and 1760 for building vast churches and mo
asteries. However, not all this building was done entirel
ad majorem Dei gloriam. Did a monastery like Wei
garten near the lake of Constance really need these fa
stretched, elegantly curved outbuildings which appear in
re-building scheme of 1723 (fig. 42)? This scheme w

never carried out; but others—e.g., at Klosterneuburg, St. Florian and Melk, all three on the Danube—were. Melk was begun in 1702 by Jacob Prandtauer (died 1726); it is in many ways the most remarkable of the three (pl. XXXIII B), shooting up out of the rocks, steep above the river. The church with its undulating front, its two many-pinnacled towers and its bulbous spires is set back. Two pavilions of the monastery buildings, housing the Marble Hall and the Library, jut forward to its right and left converging as they approach the front bastion. They are here connected by lower roughly semi-circular wings. Between these, exactly in line with the church, is an oddly Palladian arch to keep the vista open from the West portal towards the river. It is an exquisite piece of visual calculation—a late and subtle development of Palladio's so much simpler connecting of villa and landscape, and evidently the work of the century which discovered landscape gardening (see p. 187).

But, to return to our question, while the towering church on the cliff—a Durham of the Baroque—may be rightly considered a monument of militant catholicism, the palaces for abbot and monks with their richly ornamented saloons and their terraces are amenities of this world, on exactly the same level, and planned and executed in exactly the same lavish manner, as the contemporary palaces of the secular and clerical rulers of the innumerable states of the Holy Roman Empire or the country palaces of the English aristocracy, or Caserta, the palace of the King of Naples, or Stupinigi, the palace of the Duke of Savoy and King of Sardinia.

One of the most irresponsible of these schemes is the Zwinger in Dresden, built by Mathäus Daniel Pöppelmann 1662–1736) for the Elector Augustus the Strong, athlete, glutton and lecher. The Zwinger (pl. XXXIII A) is a combined orangery and Electoral grandstand for tournaments and pageants. It was not supposed to stand on its own, as it does now, attached only to the 19th-century picture gallery; it was meant to form part of a palace stretching across to the river Elbe. It consists of one-storeyed galleries with two-storeyed pavilions between. The galleries are comparatively restrained in design, but the most exuberant decoration is lavished over the pavilions. Especially the gate pavilion is a fantasy unchecked by any consideration of use. The ground-floor archway has instead of a proper pediment two bits of a broken pediment swinging away from each other. The first-floor pediment is broken too, but nodding inward instead of outward. The whole first floor is open on all sides—a kiosk or gazebo, as it were, and above its attic

GROUND FLOOR.   FIRST FLOOR.

Fig. 43.—Bruchsal, Episcopal Palace. The central staircase by
Balthasar Neumann, 1732.

swarming with figures of putti is a bulbous cupola with the Royal and Electoral emblems on top.

If those who can admire a Gothic Devon screen fee repelled by the Zwinger, they either do not really look at the object before them, or they look at it with the blinkers o puritanism. What an exultation in these rocking curves and yet what a grace. It is joyful, but never vulgar vigorous, boisterous perhaps, but never crude. It is of an inexhaustible creative power, with ever new combinations and variations of Italian Baroque forms placed against each other and piled above each other. The forward and backward motion never stops. Borromini appears massive against this swiftness of movement through space.

As in every original style, the same formal intention seems, in the German Rococo, to model space and volume. The three-dimensional curve is the *leitmotif* of the period. It appears at Vierzehnheiligen as it appears in the Zwinger, and it pervades buildings from their main theme of composition down to the smallest ornamental details. Nowhere else perhaps can this be seen as convincingly as in one of Neumann's secular masterpieces, the staircase of the Bishop's Palace at Bruchsal (pl. xxxv A and fig. 43). The palace itself is not by Neumann. It was in quite an advanced state, when in 1732 Neumann was called in to redesign the staircase.

The palace consists of a rectangular centre block or *corps de logis* and lower projecting wings, i.e., the Palladian scheme which had from Northern Italy spread to England and also to France, where it had been modified and then, in its revised shape with the space between the wings treated as a formal *cour d'honneur*, taken over by Germany. In the centre of the *corps de logis* is the staircase, an oval room, larger than any other in the palace (fig. 36). This alone is a most significant fact.

In the Middle Ages staircases had mattered little. They were nearly always tucked away—a purely utilitarian part of the building. Newel staircases taking up as little space as possible were the rule. The very latest phase of the Gothic style with its new appreciation of space had sometimes tried to endow them with spatial expression. A proper show however was only made of staircases when Italian splendour had revealed to the peoples of the West the crabbed tightness of mediæval forms. Then the French of Francis I's time could enjoy the exterior newel staircase of Blois (pl. xxxvi B) and the splendid interior double newel staircase—two parallel spirals within the same well—in the centre of the symmetrical palace of Chambord, and the Spanish, bolder still, could create shortly after 1500 a new type of staircase to be of the greatest influence in the centuries to come: the squared-up newel staircase, with three straight flights of steps around a spacious open well and the landing on the fourth side (fig. 44). This type occurs for the first time in Enrique

Fig. 44.—Enrique de Egas: Staircase in the Holy Cross Hospital, Toledo, 1504–14.

de Egas's hospital of the Holy Cross at Toledo (1504–1514) and in Michele Carlone's castle of Lacalahorra (1508–1512). Now Michele Carlone came from Genoa, and it has often been said that Genoa, where wide and airy staircases open towards courtyards became the happy rule in the later 16th century, were the inventors of this influential type. No case has however yet been pointed out quite as early as the first Spanish examples. Moreover, Spanish architects also seem to have conceived the other most spectacular Baroque type of staircase, and conceived it as early as the 1560's (fig. 53). This type, which runs in a large oblong cage, starting with two straight arms and then, after turning by 180 degrees at the landing, leads up to the upper floor in one arm between the two below (or starting with one and continuing with two), appears to my knowledge for the very first time in Juan Bautista de Toledo's and Francisco de Herrera's Escorial (1563–1584). It is eminently characteristic that these staircases, in which space is experienced most vividly by those who ascend them or descend them, originated outside Italy. The Italian Renaissance had no use for them, no use for this flow of spatial strata or compartments into one another. The best Italian Renaissance staircases, such as the one in the Palazzo Farnese (fig. 32), were comfortably wide, but led up between solid walls. Bramante's most interesting staircase, in the Vatican Palace, was of the traditional newel type, though with a wide open well and of gentle rise and generous measurements. Serlio and Palladio followed Bramante in this, although they knew and used the Spanish square three-flight type. However their hearts were not in staircase design. The only innovation in their books which is worth noting because it is so characteristically Mannerist is the newel staircase elongated into an oval shape (Maderna incidentally kept to this in the Barberini Palace (fig. 37)). The Baroque of the 17th century, especially in France, enriched the current types (see page 181). That of the Escorial became in many variations the hall-mark of princely magnificence. Neumann's Würzburg staircase with its Tiepolo paintings belongs to it.

But the staircase at Bruchsal is unique. Words can hardly re-evoke the enchanting sensation that one experiences in walking up one of its two arms.   They start in the rectangular vestibule (16 on the plan).   After about ten steps one enters the oval.   On the ground floor it is a sombre room, painted with rocks in the rustic manner of Italian grotto imitations.   The staircase itself then unfolds between two curved walls, the outside wall solid, that on the inside opened in arcades through which one looks down into the semi-darkness of the oval grotto.   The height of the arcade openings of course diminishes as the staircase ascends.   And while we walk up, it grows lighter and lighter around us, until we reach the main floor and a platform the size of the oval room beneath.   But the vault above covers the larger oval formed by the outer walls of the staircase.   Thus the platform with its balustrade separating it from the two staircase arms seems to rise in mid-air, connected only by bridges with the two principal saloons.   And the vast vault above is lit by many windows, painted with the gayest of frescoes and decorated with a splendid fireworks of stucco. The spatial rapture of the staircase is in this decoration transformed into ornamental rapture.   It culminates in the cartouche over the door leading into the Grand Saloon (pl. XXXV B).   The cartouche is not Neumann's design.   It is by a Bavarian stuccoist, Johann Michael Feichtmayr.   The contract was made in 1752.   These Bavarian stuccoists nearly all came from the same village of Wessobrunn, where boys were as a matter of course trained to become proficient in stucco work, just as the decorators of Romanesque churches so often came from certain villages round the North Italian lakes, the makers and vendors of plaster-of-Paris statuettes in the 19th century from Savoy, and the onion-men of to-day from Brittany.   Feichtmayr travelled about from job to job, and, when he worked for a monastery, still received wages and board just as the workmen did seven hundred years ago. Neumann must have met him on some job and have recognised his immense wealth of ornamental inventiveness. He appears at Vierzehnheiligen as well as at Bruchsal.   In his stucco ornament not one part is symmetrical.   The main composition is a zig-zag, from the alluring young angel on the right, up to the cupid or cherub higher up on the left, and up again to the cherub at the top.   The forms in detail seem to be incessantly changing, splashing up and sinking back. What are they? Do they represent anything? Sometimes they look like shells, sometimes like froth, sometimes like gristle, sometimes like flames. This kind of ornament— the French call it *rocaille*, and it has given the Rococo style its name—was a completely original creation, not dependent on anything of the past, as the ornament of the Renaissance had been. It is abstract art of as high an expressional value as any that we are offered to-day so much more pretentiously.

Bruchsal with its perfect unity of space and decoration is the high-water mark of the Baroque style. It is also its end. For only a few years after it had been completed and Neumann had died, Winckelmann published his first books, initiating the Classical Revival in Germany. Between Neumann's world and that of Goethe there is no link. The men of the new world no longer thought in terms of churches and palaces. No church designed anywhere after 1760 is amongst the historically leading examples of architecture. Napoleon built no palaces.

The English nobility, it must be admitted, did; right into the Victorian age. But they had nothing of the unreflecting attitude of the Baroque. This change from a style binding for all and understood by all to a style for the educated only, did not take place in Germany and Italy until 1760. In France and Britain it had come about earlier. But then neither France nor Britain (nor the North of Germany, Holland, Denmark and Scandinavia) had ever accepted the Baroque with all its implications. Their world—it is in many respects *the* modern world—is that of Protestantism. In Roman Catholic countries mediæval traditions lived and flourished down to the 18th century. In the North the Reformation had broken that happy unity. But it had also opened the way for independent thinking and feeling. The Protestant countries (and one should include here the France of the Gallicans, Jansenists and Encyclopædists) had created Puritanism, Enlightenment, the modern predominance of experimental science, and finally the Industrial Revolution in the material and the symphony in the spiritual world. What the cathedral had been to the Middle Ages, the symphony was to the 19th century.

CHAPTER SEVEN

BRITAIN AND FRANCE FROM THE 16th TO THE 18th CENTURY

At the time of Bruchsal and the *Trasparente*, large houses of Palladian or Neo-Classical style appeared all over England, houses such as Prior Park, near Bath, Holkham Hall, Stowe and Kenwood. In France meanwhile the classic grandeur of Versailles had given way to the neo-classical delicacy of the Place de la Concorde and the Petit Trianon. Evidently the development of architecture after the end of the Gothic style had been very different in Western Europe from that in Central Europe.

Yet, in Britain, France, the Netherlands, Spain and Germany, the position had been virtually the same early in the 16th century. In all these countries artists almost at the same moment turned their backs on their Gothic past, attracted by the same new style, the Italian Renaissance. Everywhere during the 15th century, the fascination of Humanism, of Roman literature and the clarity and suppleness of the classic Latin style had been experienced by scholars. The invention of printing helped to spread the new ideals, and many patrons arose among princes, noblemen and merchants. A few of these, when for some reason or other they found themselves in Italy, were converted to Italian art as well, as soon as they had understood its humanistic character. How forceful the sensation must have been it is hardly possible for us to appreciate. One keeps forgetting that it was still a time of scanty and slow communications. Perpendicular to the English, Flamboyant to the French and their national versions of Late Gothic to the Spaniards and Germans was the only architecture they knew. Now all of a sudden, when Charles VIII of France set out on his campaign against Italy in 1494, marched right across the country and captured Naples, or when Dürer, the greatest of German painters, went to Venice in the same year as a young man of twenty-three, they were faced with a style that made all they had known appear confused, crabbed and petty. At the same time, however, these airy, spacious halls, these bold square palaces, these columns, balusters and round-headed arches, these garlands and laurel wreaths and cupids were so disconcertingly novel that it took even the most progressive many years to digest them. Charles VIII, under whom the French army had first invaded Italy, died in 1498. No work of his reign survives in France in which Italian motifs occur.

But his successor Louis XII called Italian workmen into the country, and he and his court entrusted them with a good deal of decorative architectural work. The earliest existing examples are of 1506 and 1507, and exactly then Dürer went to Venice a second time, now to start embellishing his pictures and engravings with Italian ornament. Again only one or two years later Quentin Matsys, the leading artist of Antwerp, introduced Southern motifs into his works. And in 1509 Henry VII had an agreement drawn up with an Italian sculptor, Giulio Mazzini, called Paganino, who then worked at the French court, to carve his tomb. The job did not materialise, but in 1512 Henry VIII found another Italian, Pietro Torrigiani, a fellow-student of Michelangelo in Florence, to design the tomb for his father. As Torrigiani carved it, so it now stands in Henry VII's Chapel in Westminster Abbey (fig. 45), a stranger in the midst of the wonders of Gothic ingenuity that surround it. No more poignant contrast can be imagined than that between Perpendicular panels and these medallions surrounded by wreaths, Perpendicular piers and these daintily ornamented pilasters, Perpendicular mouldings and the Antique mouldings of this base and this cornice, or Perpendicular foliage and the smiling beauty of these roses and acanthus friezes.

One should however keep in mind that, when France, England, Spain and Germany discovered the loveliness of this style and made a fashion of it, it was already a style of the past in Italy.* What the architecture of 1520 was like in Rome, has been shown. Bramante, Raphael and their followers had discarded most of that pretty ornament and

* An example of Spanish Early Renaissance is Egas's Hospital of the Holy Cross at Toledo, dating from 1504–14; see fig. 44.

turned towards a grave classic ideal. For this, time was not ripe yet—in France for some twenty years, and in Britain for nearly a hundred. Early Renaissance was in full blossom this side of the Alps, when on the other side art and architecture had already passed the summit of High Renaissance. Michelangelo's Medici Chapel and Laurenziana with their Mannerist discords are earlier than the most exquisite piece of Italian decoration surviving in England, the stalls of King's College Chapel, Cambridge of 1532–36

Fig. 45.—Pietro Torrigiani: Tomb of Henry VII at Westminster Abbey, designed in 1512.

(pl. xxxvi A). Again the contrast between the only slightly older chapel itself and this addition from abroad is striking. And as the one was in the idiom with which everybody had grown up, while the other seemed to speak a foreign language, it is understandable that English patrons wavered between admiration and bewilderment. Very few were prepared to go the whole way (more in fact in France, where there was less of a racial contrast than in England), and those who did, had to rely on craftsmen from Italy, because the English or even the French mason could not at once get into a manner so novel both technically and spiritually.

Now of Italians there were more and more who found their way into France and were welcomed by Francis I, but few who travelled on to Britain. Leonardo da Vinci died in France. Primaticcio came in 1532, Serlio in 1540. They were all painters and not trained for building in the mediæval sense. They only designed and for the execution of their designs had to rely on the native master masons. A deep antagonism developed at once between the Italians and the competent traditional craftsmen of France to whom these Italian intruders were mountebanks and jacks-of-all-trades. So the new ideal of the artist-architect entered France in this interesting form of a struggle between the builder and the decorator.

However, the contrast does not often appear in actual buildings. For—again probably thanks to racial affinity—the French master masons very soon adopted the Italian vocabulary and used it to produce an essentially original style neither Gothic nor Renaissance. Two stages can be distinguished: the first that of the Loire school, the second that of Lescot's work at the Louvre. The wing of Francis I at Blois (pl. XXXVI B) was built between 1515 and about 1525. Every motif used in its decoration is of the North Italian Early Renaissance. On the other hand the facts that it is a newel staircase and that its vertical supports are scarcely disguised buttresses, are mediæval. Yet the emphasis on horizontal divisions, the even stronger emphasis on the top cornice, the comfortably gradual ascent of the staircase, and the arcaded galleries along the whole garden front prove that the designer of Blois, a Frenchman for all we know, had a feeling for what the Renaissance meant.

The attitude of English architects was characteristically different. Hampton Court had been begun in 1515 for Cardinal Wolsey. A little later Henry VIII asked Wolsey to make him a present of the palace in its unfinished state. He added to it, amongst other parts, the Great Hall (fig. 46). Now the palace with its courtyard and gate towers is just as completely in the Gothic tradition as the hall with its hammerbeam roof. Of the Italian Renaissance there is nothing but a limited number of ornamental details, the medallions with the heads of Roman emperors on the gate towers and the putti and foliage in the spandrels of the hall roof. They are competently done, but no attempt is made to bridge the gulf between English construction and Italian decoration.

Fig. 46.—Hampton Court: Great Hall, detail from the hammer-beam roof, 1533. Perhaps by Richard Rydge.

So while the first stage in the process of assimilation had been identical in Britain and France, their ways separated at the second already. The distance widened at the third. About 1540 several French architects of the younger genera-

A. Matthäus Daniel Pöppelmann: the *Zwinger*, Dresden, 1709–19. *B.* Jakob Prandtauer: the monastery of Melk on the Danube, 1702–36.

Balthasar Neumann: Vierzehnheiligen near Bamberg. Franconia,
begun 1743.

A. Balthasar Neumann: staircase of the Bishops' Palace, Bruchsal, designed 1732. *B.* Johann Michael Feichtmayr: stucco decoration, Bruchsal, 1752.

A. Cambridge: King's College Chapel, stalls, 1532–36.   B. Blois (on the Loire), the castle, wing of Francis I, 1515–c. 25.

A. Pierre Lescot: south-west pavilion, Louvre Palace, Paris, 1546.   *B.* Burghley House, Northamptonshire, centre pavilion, 1585.

A. Longleat, Wiltshire, begun 1567.   *B.* Inigo Jones: Queen's House,
Greenwich, begun 1616.

A. Pieter Post: the Mauritshuis, The Hague, 1633–35.   *B*. Francois
Mansart: Blois, 1635–38.

A. Claude Perrault: Louvre Palace, Paris, east façade, begun 1665.
B. John Wood the Elder: Prior Park, Bath, begun 1735. *C.* John
Wood the Younger: Royal Crescent, Bath, begun 1767.

tion, men born between 1505 and 1515, had returned from Rome, where they had gone to study Antiquity and Renaissance, and Serlio had begun to publish parts of his treatise on architecture in French at Lyons. Thus the façade of the Louvre towards the court designed by Pierre Lescot (died 1578) in 1546, is both classical and French (pl. XXXVII A). Italian forms are handled with ease and at the same time with a freedom which proves that they had become the architect's natural idiom. It is no hard task to trace the Italian sources of the triumphal arch motif, the niches between coupled columns, the pediments on brackets above windows, and the garlands held by cupids. But there is an agility in the presentation, a polish and a graceful splendour, that are French in the extreme. The segmental pediment especially, so sharply drawn and yet so smooth, with the two female figures holding with an inimitable rhetorical ostentation the shield with Henri II's crowned initial, would be impossible in Rome, where at that time Michelangelo placed his mighty cornice on the Farnese palace; impossible also in Northern Italy, where Palladio built the first of his serene villas and palaces, and utterly impossible in both Spain and England.

For Spain after her early welcome of the severest Italian 16th-century classicism (see page 115) had almost at once relapsed into the ornamental vagaries of her past. The austerity of the Escorial, Philip II's vast castle-monastery, with its seventeen courts and its 670 ft. of frontage without any decoration, is exceptional. What meets the traveller everywhere is the Plateresque, a wildly mixed style of Gothic, Mohammedan and Early Renaissance ingredients, spread over façades and inner walls as irresponsibly as ever. The Renaissance had evidently not yet been grasped in its meaning.

Almost the same happened in the Netherlands and Germany. An international centre such as Antwerp might put up a Town Hall (1561–65, by Cornelis Floris, fig. 47), tall, proud, square, of considered proportions and with a three-bay centre of proud Italian display. The motif of coupled columns with niches in between may have been seen by the architect in France rather than Italy, and the correct superimposition of the orders—Tuscan, Ionic, Corinthian, may have been learnt from the new Books of Orders, the publications on architectural theory (Serlio etc.). The meaning was Renaissance no doubt, though the towering gable with obelisks, scrolls and caryatid pilasters is entirely of the North. Floris handles it with discretion, but in the smaller town halls, guild halls and market halls, and the private houses of Flanders and Holland these gables, the *leitmotif* of the 16th and early 17th centuries, are over-crowded with jolly decoration. The provincial decorator-

Fig. 47.—Cornelis Floris: Antwerp Town Hall, 1561–65.

architects were not prepared to give up any of the orna-mental exuberance to which the Flamboyant of the 15th century had accustomed them. And instead of making up an *olla podrida* of Gothic and Renaissance such as the Span-ish Plateresque, they were headstrong and imaginative enough to invent a new set of decoration all their own, though originally derived from such Mannerist detail as that round the top windows of the Palazzo Massimi (pl. xxv A). It consists chiefly of somewhat stocky thick-set curves of fret-work or leather-strap appearance (fig. 48). They are sometimes flat, but more often three-dimensional and con-trasted with naturalistic garlands and caryatids. This so-

called strap-work style through engravers of ornamental
sample books (the most famous of them were by Vredeman
de Vries and appeared in 1565 and 1568) became popular
in the adjacent countries too—not in France of course, but
in Germany as well as England.

To understand Elizabethan and Jacobean architecture in
England one has to be familiar with the three sources just

Fig. 48.—Typical Flemish and Dutch strapwork ornament of the later
16th century (from the Rhineland County Hall, Leiden, 1596–98).

mentioned: the Italian Early Renaissance, the Loire style
in France, and the strap-work decoration of Flanders.
This wide-awake interest in so many foreign developments
is the æsthetic equivalent of England's new international
outlook since Queen Elizabeth, Gresham and Burghley.
However, one has also to remember all the time that a
strong Perpendicular tradition, the tradition of the picturesque, asymmetrical, stone-gabled manor house with its
mullioned windows and its extreme ornamental restraint
was still alive.   Thus English architecture between 1530 and

1620 is a composite phenomenon with French and Flemish elements prevailing, where we are near the Court, and English traditions, as soon as we get away from it.   Much of it is derivative, both in the sense of imitation and of conservatism, but occasionally a new expression is developed as original and as nationally characteristic as Lescot's Louvre.

Burghley House near Stamford is the work of William Cecil, Lord Burghley, Queen Elizabeth's trusted adviser and friend.   It is a mighty rectangle of about 160 by 200 ft. with an inner courtyard.   The central feature of this courtyard is a three-storeyed pavilion, dated 1585 (pl. XXXVII B). It is again designed on the French (though originally Italian) triumphal arch motif with the typically French niches between the coupled columns.   It has three orders, correctly applied; but on the third floor between the Corinthian columns there sits an utterly incongruous English mullioned and transomed bay window (the English have at no time been happy without bay windows) and above that the pavilion shoots out bits of strap-work and obelisks—a crop of Flemish decoration.   The analysis of style is confirmed by documentary evidence.   We know that no architect in a modern sense was wholly responsible for the building. Lord Burghley himself must have made a good many of the suggestions embodied in the design.   He represents a coming type: the architectural dilettante.   In 1568 he wrote to Paris for a book on architecture, and some years later he wrote again specifying one particular French book which he desired.   On the other hand it is also certain that workmen for Burghley came from the Netherlands and that a certain amount of work was actually done at Antwerp and then shipped to England.   Thus Flemish as well as French motifs are easily accounted for.   What is harder to understand is why this happy-go-lucky mixing up of foreign phrases with the English vernacular (the chimney-stacks are coupled Tuscan Doric columns complete with entablature) does not appear disjointed.   The England of Queen Elizabeth—this is all that can be said by way of an explanation—possessed such an overflowing vitality and was so eager to take in all that was sufficiently adventurous and picturesque and in some cases mannered that it could digest what would have caused serious trouble to a weaker age.

However while Burghley (and Wollaton Hall of 1580 and the entrance side of Hatfield of 1605–1612) are spectacular and stimulating enough, the real strength of English building lay in less outlandish designs. One of the earliest if not the earliest in an unmistakable Elizabethan style is Longleat in Wiltshire, begun in 1567 (pl. XXXVIII A). Here you find strap-work only very inconspicuously on the top balustrade. The portal is small and in the Italian style; with its Tuscan Doric columns it appears surprisingly restrained. Ornament is sparingly used. The effect is one of sturdy squareness. The roof is flat, the hundreds of many-mullioned, many-transomed windows are straight-headed, and the bay-windows project only slightly and have straight sides. This English squareness and the pre-dominance of large expanses of window creates sometimes, for instance at Hardwick Hall and even more in the garden side of Hatfield House, a curiously modern, that is 20th-century effect. More often these large windows, the windows of Perpendicular tradition, are combined with the plain customary English triangular gables. Small houses of this type are still as asymmetrical as of old, larger houses are symmetrical at least in plan, of C or E shape or if larger still developed round courtyards. There is a great deal of difference between Longleat and Burghley, but it took a William Cecil and a Raleigh, a Shakespeare and a Spenser, and many clear-minded, hard-headed and strong-bodied business-men to make up the England of Elizabeth. Yet it is one England, of one spirit and one style in building, vigorous, prolific, somewhat boastful, of a healthy and hearty sound-ness which, it is true, is sometimes coarse and sometimes dull—but never effeminate and never hysterical.

Compared with the gulf that separated buildings like Burghley House (or Audley End of 1603–16, or Hatfield House) from Inigo Jones's supreme achievements, the Queen's House at Greenwich, designed in 1616, though not completed until immediately before the Civil War, and the Banqueting House in Whitehall of 1619–22, the change in English architecture between 1500 and 1520 seems almost negligible. Only now England experienced what France had experienced before the middle of the 16th century, and experienced it far more startlingly, because Inigo Jones transplanted whole buildings of purely Italian character into England, where such men as Lescot had only transplanted features and—up to a point—the spirit that stood behind them.

Inigo Jones (1573–1652) bégan, it seems, as a painter. At the age of thirty-one he appears as a designer of costumes and stage-settings for one of the Masques which were a favourite entertainment of the court at that period. He became soon the accepted theatrical designer to the Royal Family. Plenty of drawings for Masques exist. They are brilliantly done, the costumes of that fantastic kind which the Baroque connected with ancient history and mythology, the stage-settings nearly all in the classical Italian style. Jones had, perhaps, been in Italy about 1600, interested probably more in painting and architectural decoration than in architecture proper. Then, however, the Prince of Wales made him his surveyor, i.e., architect, as did a short time later the Queen, and, in 1613, the King. So he went back to Italy, this time, we know from his sketch books, to study Italian buildings seriously. His ideal was Palladio: an edition of Palladio annotated by Jones is preserved.

Looking back from the Queen's House (pl. XXXVIII B) —a villa in the Italian sense, out at Greenwich—to Palladio's Palazzo Chierigati (pl. XXVI A), the close connection of style is evident, though nothing is copied. In fact we find nowhere in Jones's work mere imitation. What he had learned from Palladio and the Roman architects of the early 16th century, is to regard a building as a whole, organised throughout—in plan and elevation— according to rational rules. But the Queen's House has not the weight of the Roman Renaissance or Baroque palace. It was originally even less compact than Palladio's country houses, for it was not a complete block, as it is now, but consisted of two rectangles standing to the right and the left of the main Dover Road and only connected with each other by a bridge across the road—a curious, if not unique, composition of a spatially most effective openness. In contrast to this freedom in general plan, the strictest symmetry governs the grouping of the rooms. Now in Elizabethan country houses we find the decision already taken to tidy up façades into more or less complete symmetry. One may even come across sham windows, blocked windows and similar contrivances to force into outward symmetry what could not be made to match inside. For wholly symmetrical plans were still rare by 1610, although the trend towards them is unmistakable. In this Inigo Jones is the logical successor to the Jacobeans. But if one takes his elevations, their dignified plainness is in the strongest contrast to the Jacobean animation by windows of varying sizes, bay-windows, rounded and polygonal, dormer windows, gables and high-pitched roofs. The centre portion of the Queen's House with the loggia projects slightly: that is the only movement of the wall surface. The ground floor is rusticated, the top floor smooth. A balustrade sets the façade off against the sky. The windows are thoughtfully proportioned. There is no ornament anywhere but the delicately moulded cornices above the first-floor windows.

This was a principle with Inigo Jones. He wrote on Jan. 20, 1614: " Ye outward ornaments oft to be sollid, proporsionable according to the rulles, masculine and unaffected ". The character of the Queen's House could not be better described. And Jones knew that in building thus he was holding up an ideal not only in opposition to contemporary Britain but also to contemporary Rome, i.e., the Baroque. " All thes composed ornaments ", he added, " the which Proceed out of ye aboundance of dessigners and wear brought in by Michill Angell and his followers in my oppignion do not well in solid Architecture." Yet he did not despise ornament altogether. He uses it inside the Queen's House and, with luxurious exuberance, in the so-called double-cube room at Wilton House. Even there however there is nothing crowded. The form of his wreaths and garlands of flowers and fruit is compact. They fit into clear-cut panels, and never overgrow the structural divisions of a room. Again, Jones was fully aware of the contrast between his simple exteriors and his rich interiors. He wrote: " Outwarly every wyse man carrieth a graviti in

Publicke Places, yet inwardly hath his imaginacy set on fire, and sumtimes licenciously flying out, as nature hirself doeth often times stravagantly ", and demands the same attitude in a good building. And once more the way in which he puts his observation is personal to a degree inconceivable in an architect in England in Elizabethan and Jacobean days. For Inigo Jones is the first English architect in the modern sense. He achieved in this country what the earliest artist-architects had achieved in Italy at the beginning of the Renaissance. And as one is interested in Alberti or Leonardo da Vinci as individuals, so the genius of Inigo Jones makes one deplore over and over again how little is known of his personality.

Of Jones's other works—there are not many that can with any certainty be attributed to him—only two more must be mentioned. One is Lindsay House in Lincoln's Inn Fields, because with its rusticated ground floor and its giant order of pilasters above, supporting entablature and top balustrade, it is the prototype for a whole series of representational English town-houses down to the Royal Crescent at Bath (pl. XL C) and Nash's Regent's Park terraces. The other is the layout of Covent Garden with its tall houses, dignified and unadorned, open in galleries on the ground floor, which Jones had taken from a *piazza* at Leghorn (in fact Covent Garden was known in Evelyn's and Pepys's time as the Piazza), because it is the first of the regularly planned London squares. Its West side was centred on the small church of St. Paul's with its low, very grave, Antique portico, a design inspired by the Italian 16th-century books on architecture.

Now here, though only for a moment, a church had to be mentioned. For about one hundred years church architecture had all but stopped in Britain. And in France, although there are a number of interesting 16th-century churches, they are not amongst the historically leading works. The same might almost be said of the 17th century—in spite of St. Paul's Cathedral and Wren's City churches (which in point of fact owe their existence only to the misfortune of the Fire of London), and in spite of the Sorbonne church, the Val de Grâce and the Dome des Invalides in Paris. A history of 17th-century architecture, complete in its essentials, could be written without them, but never without domestic architecture.

Or at least a history of 17th-century architecture in Britain, France, Holland and the Protestant parts of Germany. In Germany a short Palladian phase coincides exactly with the time of Inigo Jones (Town Hall, Augsburg, 1610–20, by Elias Holl, 1573–1646). But as the country was not united, the movement remained local. And soon the Thirty Years' War swept away all that had recently been introduced. When the war was over, the Catholic South turned to Italy—with what superb ultimate results has been shown—and the North sought inspiration in Holland and France. For ten or twenty years in the early 17th century French and Dutch architecture looked in fact very similar. Henri IV had favoured a style of brick buildings with stone quoins and windows (Place des Vosges, Paris) that Holland took over just at the moment when France abandoned it in favour of a new classicism based on her own 16th-century traditions and a renewed perusal of the publications of Serlio and Palladio. François Mansart (1598–1664) is the great innovator of that generation, the generation of Descartes, Corneille and Poussin. In his work at Blois (1635–1638) and Maisons Lafitte (1642–1650) he proves himself one of the greatest of French architects. The *cour d'honneur* at Blois especially (pl. XXXIX B; on the extreme right a corner of Francis I's wing is just visible) is a masterpiece of civilised reticence, elegant, not very warm-hearted, yet far from pedantically correct with its two-storeyed triumphal arch and the remarkably original little semi-circular third-storey pediment above. The links backward with Lescot's age are as evident as the links forward with the smooth perfection of the Rococo *hôtel*.

This new French *noblesse* in building seems again to have attracted the attention of Holland, which just then attained the leadership of Western commercial enterprise and Western science, besides possessing more men of artistic genius than at any other period in her national existence. French influence may thus not have been necessary for Holland to convert her gayer and more homely style of 1600 into the new classicism of 1630—a style as characteristically Dutch as Mansart's style had been French. The Mauritshuis at the Hague was built by Peter Post in 1633–1635 (pl. XXXIX A). It is small for a princely residence, unpretentious with its plain brick walls and slightly projecting four-pilaster portico, and remarkably comfortable.

Such buildings in their turn influenced the England of the later 17th century. But architects, amateurs and scholars, and especially the Stuart Court, were also not blind to the glamour and the real achievements of the Paris of Colbert and Louis XIV. There was trading success on the one hand, the grandeur of absolute monarchy on the other. Hence representational architecture tended towards the Parisian, domestic architecture towards the Dutch. In Sir Christopher Wren's work inspiration from both sources can be traced. He must have studied engravings of Dutch architecture with great care, and he went to Paris personally, when he had realised that the designing and supervising of buildings was to be his main job in life. For Wren (1632–1723)—this is again characteristic of Renaissance and Baroque—had not been trained as an architect or a mason. But he was not a painter or sculptor or an engineer either. He represents yet another type, a type not so far met in this book.

Wren's father had been Dean of Windsor, his father's brother Bishop of Ely. He was sent to Westminster School. At the age of fifteen, after he had finished school, he was made an assistant demonstrator in anatomy at the College of Surgeons. Then he went up to Oxford. His main interest was science, in that curious mixed and vague sense which science still had in the mid-17th century. During the time he was at College, " that miracle of a youth ", as John Evelyn called him, put before the authorities fifty-three inventions, theories, experiments and mechanical improvements. Some of them seem trifling now, others aimed right at the central problems of astronomy, physics and engineering. In 1657 he was made professor of astronomy in London, in 1661 in Oxford. It was the moment when experimental science was just coming to the fore everywhere in Europe. In Paris the Royal Academy of Science was established. The Royal Society in London started its activities even earlier. Wren was one of its founders and most distinguished members. Newton calls him together with Huygens and Wallis " huius aetatis geometrarum facile principes ". His most important scientific work is on cycloids, the barometer and Pascal's problem. In his inaugural lecture in London he revealed a prophetic vision of nebulae as the firmaments of other worlds like ours. In 1664 he illustrated Willis's *Anatomy of the Brain*. And in 1663 he presented to the Royal Society a model for a building which he had designed at the request of Oxford University, the Sheldonian Theatre, completed in 1669. Its roof is an ingenious piece of timber engineering, but its architecture is awkward, evidently the work of a man of little designing experience. The same can be said of his second work, Pembroke Chapel, Cambridge, of 1663–66. An even earlier connection with building construction is indicated by Charles I's request to him to fortify Tangier. So architecture, engineering, physics and mathematics go hand in hand in the development of Wren's mind. The resolution to specialise in architecture may have been brought about by the Fire of London in 1666. Wren found himself a member of the Royal Commission for the re-building of the City, and very soon also the elected designer of the many new churches to be build in the City, including St. Paul's. In 1669 the King made him Surveyor General. His only important journey abroad took him not to Italy, but to Paris. That is a very significant fact. At the time of Inigo Jones's *Wanderjahre*, Paris could not have been more than a station on the way to Rome. Now Wren, in a letter, called Paris " a School of Architecture, the best probably at this Day in Europe ". The most important it certainly was. While Wren was in Paris, Louis XIV, who intended to rebuild the East parts of the Louvre, had invited Bernini to come and contribute designs. He did so, but his plans, a colossal square on the Roman pattern, examined for a few short minutes by Wren, were dropped as soon as the great man left. They were replaced by the famous East front with the colonnade which Claude Perrault (1613–1688) designed in 1665.

The choice of Perrault was characteristic. He was an amateur, a distinguished doctor, his brother was a lawyer and courtier, author of a mediocre poem on *Le Siècle de Louis le Grand*, and had in 1664 been made Inspector General of the King's buildings. In the history of French literature he is chiefly known as one of the leaders in the *Querelle des Anciens et des Modernes*. Boileau defended Antiquity, Perrault a contemporary style—which of course did not really mean more than a certain amount of freedom in applying the rules of the ancients.

Claude Perrault's Louvre front (pl. XL A) is an admirable example of this classic French attitude, and at the same time of the style that represents the age of Louis XIV. With its tall ground floor treated as a podium to raise the main floor, with the colonnade of slim coupled giant columns, its corner and middle pavilions, its top balustrade and centre pediment (instead of the high-pitched roofs which until then had been employed without exception), it is a brilliant adaptation of features from various sources. The general block shape may be an effect of Bernini's stay, the idea of a large first-floor loggia goes back to Palladio, individual motifs which strike one as particularly French such as the segment-headed windows or the oval shields with garlands hanging down from them, come direct from Lescot's work on the Louvre a hundred years earlier. They are motifs not authorised by the ancients or Serlio and Palladio, and the coupling of columns as well as their grouping into a triumphal arch rhythm in the central pavilion were considered most daring by contemporary critics.

The whole is of a grandeur and yet a precise elegance that the 17th century, in spite of Blois and Maisons, had never before achieved, and that the architects of Louis XIV's later years never surpassed. Perrault has summed up to perfection the various, sometimes seemingly contradictory tendencies of the *siècle de Louis XIV*, the gravity and *raison* of late Poussin, Corneille and Boileau, the restrained fire of Racine, the lucid grace of Molière, the powerful sense of organisation of Colbert.

It is necessary for an appreciation of this style to remember the atmosphere in which it grew, the struggles first between Protestantism and Catholicism in the 16th century, Henri IV's decision to return to the Roman church, because, as he put it, " Paris is worth a mass ", then the spreading of religious indifference, until it became all-powerful in the policy of Richelieu, the cardinal, and Father Joseph, the Capuchin, who fought Protestants in France but favoured them abroad, in both cases purely for reasons of national expediency. For the centre of their thoughts and ambitions was France, and a strong and prosperous France could only be created by first building up a rigorously centralised administration. Now the only visible symbol of the might of the State could be the person of the King. Absolutism was therefore the appropriate form of government for whoever was in favour of a national policy. Thus Richelieu prepared the ground for absolutism, Mazarin followed, and Colbert, the indefatigable, competent and tenacious bourgeois, made a system of it. He organised France with an unheard-of thoroughness: mercantilism in industry and commerce, Royal workshops, Royal trading companies, close supervision of roads, of canals, of afforestation—of everything.

Art and architecture were an integral part of the system. A flourishing school of painting, sculpture and the applied arts stimulated export and at the same time enhanced the glory of the court. Architecture was useful to create work and again to celebrate the greatness of King and State. But there should be no licence; style had to conform to standards set by the prince and his minister. Thus academies were founded, one for painting and sculpture, another for architecture, the earliest of a modern type, both educational and representational, and the most powerful that have ever existed. And when artists had gone through these schools and gained distinction, they were made Royal sculptors or Royal architects, drawn nearer and nearer to the court, honoured and paid accordingly, but made more and more dependent on the will of Louis and Colbert. It was in Paris at that time that the principle of architecture as a department of the civil service was established. The French and English Kings had had their Royal master masons ever since the 13th century. But they were craftsmen, not civil servants. Also the competencies of the various surveyors, inspectors and whatever they were called later on, were never clearly defined. Michelangelo had been Superintendent of the Papal Buildings; but nobody would have considered such an appointment a full-time job. Now the architectural office developed, and a system of training at the drawing board and on the jobs.

Jules Hardouin-Mansart (1646–1708) was the perfect type of the official French architect, competent, quick and adaptable. In his church of St. Louis des Invalides (pl. XLI A) of 1675–1706 he achieved, just as Perrault did, that specific combination of grandeur and elegance which is not to be found anywhere outside France. The portico has two orders, Doric with a correct frieze, and Ionic. But the free rhythmical spacing of the columns is taken over from Perrault. The tall drum of the dome has segment-headed, strikingly domestic-looking windows, the lantern a free, graceful and completely un-Antique shape. The interior is on a central plan, but the dome is constructed so that in looking up one sees through a wide opening in the inner cupola on to the painted surface of a second cupola, lit by concealed windows—a wholly Baroque spatial effect. Returning to the façade one will now become aware of its Baroque qualities too, the graded advance in plan towards the centre: first step from the walls to the columns of the wings, second step to the columns on the sides of the portico, and third step to the four middle columns. Not only the Greeks but also Palladio would have deprecated this strongly.

Sir Christopher Wren did not. His St. Paul's Cathedral of 1675–1710 (pl. XLI B and fig. 49) though apparently so much a monument to Classicism is in fact just as much a blend of the classical and the Baroque as the Dôme des Invalides. The dome of St. Paul's, one of the most perfect in the world, is classical indeed. It has a more reposeful outline than Michelangelo's and Hardouin-Mansart's. The decoration with a colonnade round the drum is also characteristically different from the projecting groups of columns and broken entablatures of St. Peter's and

St. Louis's. But looking more closely, even there the alternation of bays where columns flank niches, with bays where they stand in front of loggias, introduces an element of unclassical variety. The lantern, too, is just as bizarre as Mansart's. And as for the façade of St. Paul's, begun in 1685, it is, with the coupled columns which Wren took over from Perrault's Louvre façade, and the two fantastic turrets on the sides (designed after 1700), a decidedly Baroque composition. The side elevations are dramatic, though of a secular, palace-like effect. The windows have even a framing of sham-perspective niches

Fig. 49.—Sir Christopher Wren: St. Paul's Cathedral, 1675–1710.

of the S. Carlo and Palazzo Barberini type (see pl. xxix B). Inside there is a poignant contrast between the firmness of every part and the spatial dynamics of the whole. The dome rests on diagonally placed piers with colossal niches hollowed out. Niches also set the outer walls of the aisles and choir aisles into an undulating motion. With a similar effect windows are cut into the barrel vaults and saucer domes of choir and nave. Wren's style in churches and palaces is Palladian, no doubt, but it is a Baroque version of Classicism. Such city churches as the ingeniously multiform St. Stephen's, Walbrook (1672–1687, pl. xlii and fig. 50), show this especially clearly.

To analyse its ground plan is almost as hard as to analyse Vierzehnheiligen. Yet its expression is of cool clarity. Outside it is a plain rectangle as silent about the interior surprises as Vierzehnheiligen. Inside its centre is a spacious gently rising saucer dome resting on eight arches supported by nothing but twelve slender columns. The technical achievement is as remarkable as the effortless lightness of appearance. The twelve columns form a square, and four arches connect the two central columns of each side of the square, while fragmentary vaults curve up from the three columns of each corner of the square to form four more

Fig. 50.—Sir Christopher Wren: St. Stephen's, Walbrook, London, 1672–87. Length inside 83 ft.

arches in the corners. Now, these three corner columns on each side are also tied together by straight entablatures so that each of the four sides has a rhythm of straight and low—arched and tall—straight and low. Here is a first ingenious interlocking of effects. Looking up the dome we perceive eight arches of identical height, but looking straight in front of us towards any one side of the square there is differentiation of the bays. However, that is not all. The arched centres of the sides can also be regarded as the entrances to four arms of a cross, a Latin cross, since the barrel-vaults of the South and North arms are very shallow, whereas the East arm with the altar has a somewhat longer cross-vault, and the West arm one double the length of the altar arm. To achieve that, the Western arm consists of two bays separated by columns in the normal manner of longitudinal churches. As these columns are exactly identical with all the other columns, the first impression one receives on entering the church is one of a short nave with aisles leading towards a dome of unaccountable width. To finish the story, this seeming nave has narrow flat-ceilinged outer aisles as well, and these outer aisles run right through to the East wall. Only we cannot call them aisles all the way through, because at one point they rise into being the North and South arms of the cross and then sink again to become chancel aisles. The inner aisles of course, one discovers later, run into the wide crossing just as the nave. The whole rectangle of the church is set out with sixteen columns altogether, noble columns of almost academic neutrality. Yet they are used to create a spatial polyphony which only the Baroque could appreciate —architecture of Purcell's age.

It is in connection with the spatial qualities of his ground plans that one should consider Wren's plan for the re-building of London after the fire of 1666. He suggested sweeping alterations in the pattern of the city, new long, wide and straight streets meeting in star-shaped squares. Now this principle of the *rond-point* with radiating streets originated from the Italy of the Renaissance (see p. 97), was put into practice by the Mannerists—the most famous example is Scamozzi's octagonal town and fortress of Palmanova in the Veneto (1593)—and then taken over late in the 16th century by the French under Louis XIV. France (where the radiating chapels of the church plan had been conceived six hundred years before) became the second home of the *rond-point*. Louis' reign dates the Place de l'Étoile, although it was then in the country and became part of the city of Paris only after 1800. The grandest example of such planning on an enormous scale is, of course, Versailles (fig. 51). The garden front of the palace, 1,800 feet long, faces Le Nôtre's magnificent park with its vast parterres of flowers, its cross-shaped sheet of water, fountains, seemingly endless parallel or radiating avenues, and walks between tall trimmed hedges—Nature subdued by the hand of Man to serve the greatness of the King, whose bedroom was placed right in the centre of the whole composition. On the town side the *cour d'honneur* receives three wide converging roads coming from the direction of Paris. Town-planning was strongly influenced by these principles everywhere. Of the 18th century the most notable examples are perhaps Karlsruhe in South-West Germany, a whole town designed in 1715 as one huge

Fig. 51.—Versailles. The garden front by Jules Hardouin-Mansart, 1676–88, the gardens by André Le Nôtre, begun 1667.

star with the Ducal Palace as its centre, and L'Enfant's plan of 1791 for Washington, D.C.

As for Britain, Wren's plan fell through after having been considered by the King for only a few days. Was it too daring? Could it have been carried out only in an absolute monarchy, where expropriation for schemes of civic grandeur was easier than in the City of London? Or was this logical, uncompromising programme to organise the background for future London life simply too un-English ever to be taken seriously? The fact remains that the contribution of London to town-planning of the 17th and 18th centuries is the square—introduced, as has been said, by Inigo Jones—i.e., an isolated, privately owned area with houses of, as a rule, similar but not identical design, examples of good manners and not of regimentation. It might be worth adding that the sensation in walking through the West-end of London from square to square is clearly a modern and secular version of the typically English sensation of the visitor passing from isolated compartment to isolated compartment in a Saxon or Early English church.

Regarding the individual town house, there is the same contrast between London and Paris. In London, but for a few exceptions, the nobleman and the wealthy merchant lived in terrace houses, in Paris in detached *hôtels*. In London a ground plan had been evolved for these houses that was convenient enough to become standardised before the end of the 17th century. With its entrance on one side, leading straight to the staircase, one large front room and one large back room on each floor, and the service rooms in the basement, it remained practically unaltered for the largest and the smallest house until the end of the Victorian era. Of spatially effective elements it has little. In Paris, on the other hand, architects from the middle of the 17th century invented an infinite variety of modifications of the *hôtel* ground plan, based as a rule on the arrangement with a *cour d'honneur*, screened off from the street, with service rooms and stables in wings on the right and the left, and the *corps de logis* at the back. The principal rooms overlooked a garden behind the house. Inexhaustible ingenuity was displayed in finding ever new groupings (fig. 52). One difficulty that the architects had often to overcome was that the front and the back should both be symmetrical and yet did not lie on the same axis. The subtlest solutions were devised in the 18th century, as graceful as the contemporary ornament of the *rocaille* (which the French—as against the Germans—never allowed to flow over into exterior decoration). Small *antichambres* and *garderobes* were fitted into the spare corners behind curved and polygonal rooms. The form and position of the staircase was another problem. As to its position, it had to communicate easily with vestibule and service rooms, without interfering with the smooth run of room into room and the representational splendour of vistas. The same desire for a smooth run was extended to the interaction between floor and floor, and staircase forms were chosen accordingly. It has been shown that Spain, for all we know, invented both

Fig. 52.—Jean Courtonne: Hôtel Matignon, Paris, 1726.

the most popular types of Baroque staircases (fig. 53). The square one with three flights round an open well became popular in Jacobean England, where it was interpreted in timber, characteristically reduced in size to a somewhat cramped mediæval narrowness, but gorgeously decorated by Flemish or English woodcarvers (Hatfield, Audley End, etc.). Only when we come to Inigo Jones at Ashburnham House,

London (probably by him), is the spaciousness of Spain emulated. However, Ashburnham House and a few other examples of Baroque breadth such as Coleshill, Berks, are rare exceptions in England. There are at that time exceptions in Italy too (Longhena: S. Giorgio Maggiore, Venice, 1643–45 —the example from which Coleshill seems to be derived). Only Genoa took a real liking to staircases as wide, light and airy as those of Spain. France must have got to know of these through several channels. The Escorial type was taken up by Mansart at Blois and by Levau at the Tuileries in Paris. Since then it was established as the grandest of all types. The square open-well type occurs with countless minor variations in Paris *hôtels* (see e.g., fig. 52). These variations all aim at suppler, more elegant forms.

Fig. 53.—Two chief types of Baroque staircases.

Externally the Paris *hôtels* are just as elegantly varied, whereas in London the exterior of the 17th- and 18th-century brick house was, except for ornamental details, almost standardised. It has no connection with the classic French style, that much is certain, although it may have had some originally with the less pretentious domestic architecture of Henri IV and later with Holland.

As for country houses, they are—at least after 1660—of minor importance in France, where the life of the ruling class was centred in the court, while in England most of the noblemen and nearly all the squires still regarded their London houses only as *pieds-à-terre*, and looked on their seats in the country as their real homes. Consequently it is here that one can expect variety and, indeed, finds it. All the more noteworthy, however, is it that about 1700, when the standardised town house had become an accepted fact, a type of smaller country house had also been introduced (clearly on the Mauritshuis pattern) that—with many and delightful minor variations—is to be found all over the countryside, in the villages round London, at Hampstead, Roehampton, Ham, Petersham, round the close at Salisbury—everywhere. They are usually built of brick with stone quoins, either com-

Fig. 54.—Fenton House, Hampstead, 1693.

pletely rectangular or with two short wings on the sides, the entrance with a pediment, hood or porch, and with a larger pediment to crown the centre of the house (fig. 54). These lovable houses of mellow and undated rightness are too well known to need further description. Their interiors are simple and straightforward; of that ingenious *commodité* on which all the French 18th-century architects insisted in their writings, they have little.

Apparently, to the British, comfort was something quite

different from what it was to the French. But while these houses of about 1700 are, whatever French critics might have said against them, as serviceable to-day as at the time when they were built, there are indeed certain English 18th-century country houses on a larger scale which—from our point of view at least—seem to be designed for display and not for comfort. This is an argument heard frequently against Blenheim near Oxford (pl. XLII B, XLIII A, XLIV B and fig. 55), the palace which the nation presented to Marlborough. It was designed by Sir John Vanbrugh (1664–1726) in 1705. His style derives from Wren at his grandest and most

Fig. 55.—Sir John Vanbrugh: Blenheim Palace, begun 1705.
Total width *c.* 850 ft.

Baroque—the Wren of Greenwich Hospital—but is always of a distinctly personal character. Wren never seems to forget himself. He is never carried away by forces stronger than his reason. Vanbrugh's designs are of a violence and ruthless directness that could not but offend the rationalists of his age. His family came from Flanders; his expansive temperament seems more of Rubens's country than of Wren's and Reynolds's. He studied art in France, was arrested and put into the Bastille. After his release he returned to England and began to write plays. They were a huge success. Then suddenly one finds him engaged in architectural work at Castle Howard. In 1702 he was appointed Comptroller of Works—a curious career, very different from Wren's.

Blenheim is planned on a colossal scale. One does not know whether the Palladian villa with its wings or Versailles with its *cour d'honneur* stands behind its plan. The *corps de logis* has a massive portico with giant columns between giant pillars, and a heavy attic above. The same Baroque weight characterises the side elevations, especially the square squat corner towers of the wings (pl. XLIII A). If in the case of Wren the term Baroque could be used only with careful qualifications, these towers would be called Baroque by anyone familiar with the work of Bernini, Borromini and the others in Italy. Here is struggle, mighty forces opposing overwhelming weights; here are fiercely projecting mouldings and windows crushed by thick-set pilasters placed too close to them; here is the deliberate discordance of the semi-circular window placed against a semi-circular arch right above and higher up again a segmental arch. Everything jars, and the top of the daring composition has nothing of a happy end either. Vanbrugh in the forms which crown the tower, the obelisks and the ball, does not accept any indebtedness to anybody. The pilasters and the windows are also highly original, but not to the same extreme degree. In some details they appear reminiscent of Michelangelo. However, the mentioning of Michelangelo makes Blenheim —the whole of the entrance front—at once appear coarse, even meaty, and certainly theatrical and ostentatious: that is Flemish as well as Baroque. Yet in spite of that Vanbrugh, seen side by side with Michelangelo or Bernini, is also a classicist. It seems a contradiction but it is not. It simply is, just as in the case of Wren, the special English twist given to the Baroque. There is very little in Wren and Vanbrugh of that plastic treatment of walls which Michelangelo had first conceived and which produced the undulating façades and interiors of Baroque buildings in Italy and Southern Germany. Movement is never in England so insinuating, nor so frantic. Spatial parts never abandon their separate existence, to merge into each other, as they do at S. Carlo or Vierzehnheiligen. The individual members, especially the solid round detached columns, also try to keep themselves to themselves. Vanbrugh's drama lies in the visible forcing of this English aloofness into the service of an overmighty plan. English Baroque is Baroque asserting itself against an inborn leaning towards the static and the sober.

The same conflict will be experienced in interiors of Wren's and Vanbrugh's time. There again spatial relations bind rooms together which are articulated and decorated according to the principles of Classicism—by panelling, if they are small, by columns or pilasters, if they are larger. At Blenheim there is an enormous entrance hall leading into the saloon which forms the centre of two symmetrical groups of rooms along the whole garden front, with all the doors in one axis, or, as it is called, one *enfilade*, as at Versailles. But— this is of the greatest significance—the staircase, the dynamic element *par excellence*, is nothing like as prominent as it would be in a contemporary palace in France or Germany. This lack of interest in spatial dynamics is by no means a sign of meanness in planning. On the contrary, Blenheim is just as vast as the largest new palaces of the minor rulers of Germany, and just as unpractical—at least from our point of view.

However, it seems rather cheap to harp on the fact that kitchen and service rooms are far away from the dining room—in one of the two wings in fact, opposite the other with the stables (an accepted Palladian tradition). Servants may have had to walk a long way, and hot dishes may have got cold long before they reached their destination. To us that may seem a functional error. Vanbrugh and his clients would have called such arguments extremely low. Of servants one had plenty. And what we call comfort mattered less than a self-imposed etiquette more rigid than we can imagine. The function of a building is not only utilitarian. There is also an ideal function, and that Blenheim did fulfil. However, not all Vanbrugh's contemporaries agreed that it did. There is e.g. Pope with his famous, often quoted "'tis very fine, But where d'ye sleep, or where d'ye dine?" What did he mean by that? Critics to-day interpret it as referring to a lack of material comfort. Pope was more philosophical than that. What, in the name of good sense, he asked for, is that a room and a building should look what they are. He disliked Vanbrugh's colossal scale and decorative splendour as unreasonable and unnatural. For " splendour ", he insists, should borrow " all her rays from sense ", and again:

> " Something there is more needful than expense,
>   And something previous e'en to taste—'tis sense."

In this he gave expression to the feelings of his generation, the generation following Vanbrugh's. For Pope was born in 1688, whereas Vanbrugh was of almost the same age as Swift and Defoe (and Wren as Dryden).

The architecture that corresponds to Pope's poetry is that of Lord Burlington and his circle. Richard Boyle, Earl of Burlington, was some years younger than Pope. He went to Italy at the age of twenty, and when he came back, brought with him several artists and architects attached to him by a common admiration of Palladio. Already in 1715 a sumptuous English edition of Palladio had been published by the Italian architect Leoni; now Burlington paid for Colin Campbell's *Vitruvius Britannicus* consisting of illustrations of the best modern buildings in Britain (1715–25), and the publication of Inigo Jones's works by William Kent, painter, landscape gardener and architect (1727). These publications set a Palladian fashion in British country houses that lasted almost unchallenged for fifty years, and with certain modifications for nearly a hundred.

The town house, however, was hardly affected. There are very few examples of Palladian influence beyond façade motifs. And where, as in a house designed by Lord Burlington himself, an attempt was made to interfere with the standardised London plan, the outcry against this imposition of the rationalist's new rules was just as pronounced as the rationalist's outcry had been against Vanbrugh's unruliness. Lord Chesterfield suggested to the owner that he should take a house opposite, so as to be able to admire his own at leisure without having to live in it.

It is the country house that became wholly Palladian by Lord Burlington's efforts. In Vanbrugh's work the variety of plans and exterior compositions had been unlimited. Now the *corps de logis* with a centre portico and isolated wings connected to the main body by low galleries became *de rigueur*. Prior Park, near Bath (pl. XL B), is a typical example. It was designed for Ralph Allen in 1735 by the elder John Wood (*c.* 1700–1754), a local architect, but, by virtue of his talent and the opportunities which he had in the most fashionable spa of England, one of the leading architects of his generation. Compared with Palladio's villas, these British derivations are larger and heavier. They also often incorporate motifs freer than Palladio would have tolerated: more variation in the shapes of rooms, or a boldly curved outer staircase into the garden (the one at Prior Park is of the 19th century). The sites, as a rule on a gentle slope, also add a quality that is absent in Palladio's work for a flat country. But more important still is the fact that Palladian country houses in Britain were designed to stand in English parks.

It seems at first contradictory that the same patrons should have wanted the formal Palladian house and the informal English garden, and that the same architect should have provided both. Yet it is a fact that William Kent, Lord Burlington's protégé, was celebrated as one of the creators of the English style in laying out grounds, and that Lord Burlington's own Villa at Chiswick (about 1720), a free copy of Palladio's Villa Rotonda, was one of the earliest examples of what was called " the modern taste " in gardening. How can this have come about? Was the landscape garden just a whim? It was not; it was a conscious part of an anti-French policy in the arts. Le Nôtre's parks express absolutism, the King's absolute rulership over the country, and also Man's rulership over Nature. The active, expansive Baroque force that shapes the house, flows over into nature. Progressive English thinkers recognised this and disliked it. Shaftesbury spoke of " the mockery of princely gardens ", and Pope satirised them in his neat couplet:

> " Grove nods at grove, each alley has a brother,
> And half the platform just reflects the other."

Now this enforcing of architectural rule on the garden is

certainly something unnatural.   And so Addison wrote in *The Spectator* in 1712: " For my own part I would rather look upon a tree in all its luxuriance and diffusion of boughs and branches than when it is cut and trimmed into a mathematical figure ".   That profession of faith in nature not tampered with is evidently a revolt of liberalism and tolerance against tyranny; it is a Whig revolt.   But the curious thing about it is that although these attacks were made in the name of nature, nature was still understood by Addison and Pope in Newton's and indeed in Boileau's sense.   Boileau's objections in his *Art of Poetry* of 1674 against the Baroque of the South were that it was unreasonable and therefore unnatural.   Reason and nature are still synonyms with Addison and Pope, as we have seen in Pope's comments on Blenheim.

Add to this Shaftesbury's " passion for things of a natural kind " and his idea that " the conceit or caprice of Man has spoiled their genuine order by breaking in upon (their) primitive state ", and you will be near an answer to the puzzling parallelism between classicist architecture and natural gardening.   The original state of the universe is harmony and order, as we see it in the ordered courses of the stars which were revealed by the new telescopes, and in the structures of organisms which were revealed by the new microscopes.   " Idea or Sense, Order, Proportion everywhere ", to use Shaftesbury's words once more.   Now to illustrate the superiority of harmony over chaos Shaftesbury explicitly refers to the superiority of the " regular and uniform pile of some noble Architect " over " a Heap of Sand or Stones ".   But is not the heap of sand nature in her primitive state?   That the early 18th century did not want to recognise.   So we arrive at this curious ambiguity.   Simple nature is order and harmony of proportion.   So a natural architecture is an architecture according to Palladio.   But simple nature is also, in the common speech of everybody, fields and hedgerows, and of these people were genuinely fond, at least in England.   So the garden should be left as close to this simple nature as possible.   Addison was the first to reach this conclusion.   He exclaimed: " Why may not a whole estate be thrown into a kind of garden ", and

" A man might make a pretty landscape of his own possessions ". Pope followed Addison in a contribution to *The Guardian* in 1713 and, more important still, in his own miniature garden at Twickenham. However, when it came to " improving " Twickenham (to use the 18th-century term) in 1719–1725—another equally remarkable thing happened. These earliest anti-French gardens were by no means landscape gardens in the later sense. They were not Pope's " Nature unadorned ". Their plans with elaborately meandering paths and rills are of as artificial an irregularity as Baroque regularity had been before. Or as Horace Walpole put it in 1750: " There is not a citizen who doesn't take more pains to torture his acre and a half into irregularities than he formerly would have employed to make it as formal as his cravat." Now all that, this " twisting and twirling " (to use Walpole's words again), is evidently Rococo, and nearer in spirit to the Bruchsal Rocaille than to those gardens of the later 18th century which really tried to look like untouched nature. It is the English version of Rococo —as characteristically English as Wren's Baroque had been in comparison with Continental Baroque.

So while one remembers the grandeur and elegance of French 17th- and 18th-century architecture as urban all the way through—for the straight avenues in the park of Versailles are urban in spirit too—one should never forget in looking at the formality of English Palladian houses between 1660 and 1760 that their complement is the English garden. John Wood's Prior Park possesses such informal natural grounds. And even in the most urban developments of Georgian England such as New Edinburgh and above all Bath nature was close at hand and willingly admitted.

John Wood was the first after Inigo Jones to impose Palladian uniformity on an English square as a whole. All the squares in London and elsewhere laid out since 1660 had left it to each owner of a house to have it designed as he liked, and it was only due to the rule of taste in Georgian society that not one of these houses ever violently clashed with its neighbours. John Wood now made one palace front with central portico and secondary emphasis on the corner blocks out of his Queen Square in Bath.

That was in 1728.   Twenty-five years later he designed the
Circus (1754–*c.* 1770), again as a uniform theme.   His son,
the younger John Wood (died 1781), in the Royal Crescent
of 1767–*c.* 1775 (pl. XL C) broke open the compactness of
earlier squares and ventured to provide as the only response
to his vast semi-elliptical palace frontage of thirty houses
with giant Ionic columns a spacious, gently sloping lawn.
Here the extreme opposite of Versailles has been reached.
Nature is no longer the servant of architecture.   The two
are equals.   The Romantic Movement is at hand.

In London the principle of the palace façade for a whole
row of houses was introduced by Robert Adam in his
Adelphi (that magnificent composition of streets with its
Thames front known all over Europe, which was destroyed,
not by bombs, but by mercenary Londoners just before the
war) and then taken up at Fitzroy Square and Finsbury
Square.   But Adam's work, which won international fame
in the sixties and seventies—at the same moment when the
English garden also began to influence Europe—should not
be discussed so close to the Palladianism of the Burlington
group.   It is of a fundamentally different kind.   As a rule
this difference is expressed by placing Adam at the beginning
of the so-called Classical Revival.   But that is not the whole
answer, for the Classical Revival is really only a part of a
much wider process, the Romantic Movement.   So from the
renewed direct approach to Greek and Roman antiquities as
well as from the English creation of landscape gardening we
are led into a consideration of the central European problem
of 1760–1830: the Romantic Movement.

CHAPTER EIGHT

ROMANTIC MOVEMENT, HISTORICISM AND MODERN MOVEMENT

(FROM 1760 TO THE PRESENT DAY)

THE Romantic Movement originated in England. In literature this fact is well enough known. For the arts and for architecture in particular it has yet to be established. In literature Romanticism is the reaction of sentiment against reason, of nature against artificiality, of simplicity against pompous display, of faith against scepticism. Romantic poetry expresses a new enthusiasm for nature and a self-abandoning veneration of the whole, elemental, undoubting life of early or distant civilisations. This veneration led to the discovery of the Noble Savage and the Noble Greek, the Virtuous Roman and the Pious Mediæval Knight. Whatever its object, the Romantic attitude is one of longing, that is antagonism to the present, a present which some saw predominantly as Rococo flippancy, others as unimaginative rationalism, and others again as ugly industrialism and commercialism.

The opposition to the present and the immediate past goes through all utterances of the Romantic spirit, although certain tendencies within the new movement grew out of the 18th century's Rationalism and Rococo. It has been shown for instance how the conception of the landscape garden—a truly Romantic conception—dates back to Addison and Pope, but appears at first in Rococo dress. Similarly that most popular architectural expression of Romanticism, the revival of mediæval forms, started long before the Romantic Movement proper and went through all the phases of 18th-century style, before it became wholly Romantic in character.

In fact the Gothic style had never quite died in England. There is College work in Oxford of the 17th century which is unselfconscious Perpendicular, notably the staircase up to the hall of Christ Church College. Wren also used Gothic forms in some of the London City churches, and others followed him. But the beginnings of an original handling of mediæval elements, a revival and not a survival, are connected with Vanbrugh and his school. His own house at Blackheath of 1717–1718 is castellated and has a fortified-looking round tower. He also introduced castellated structures into some of the grounds which he furnished or laid out. His reason for doing so was that mediæval forms suggested strength, and he always wanted to be *masculine* in his designs. Hence thick round towers and battlements occur even in his country houses which are otherwise in the current style. However, it was not only their æsthetic qualities which tempted him in mediæval castles. He saw more in them. Not that he actually built sham ruins as the later 18th century did, but he defended the preservation of genuine ruins when he found them, because they " move lively and pleasing reflections . . . on the persons who have inhabited them (and) on the remarkable things which have been transacted in them ", and because " with yews and hollies in a wild thicket " they make " one of the most agreeable objects that the best of landscape painters can invent ".

Vanbrugh's austere version of mediævalism found no successors, but the two passages quoted from his memorandum of 1709 on Blenheim form the foundation of Romantic Revivalism. As will have been noticed Vanbrugh uses two arguments: the associational and the picturesque. Both were developed by theorists of the 18th century. A building is clothed in the garb of a special style, because of the meditations which that style will rouse. And a building is conceived in conjunction with the surrounding nature, because the virtuosi had discovered on the Grand Tour amid the ruins of Roman architecture in and around Rome, the truth and the picturesqueness of the heroic and idyllic landscapes of Claude Lorraine, Poussin, Dughet and Salvator Rosa. These were bought freely by English collectors and helped to form the taste of artists and gardeners, amateur and professional.

Lorraine may have been admired by Pope and Kent (who after all was a painter before he became an architect), but the gardens of Twickenham and Chiswick had nothing of

A. Jules Hardouin-Mansart: St. Louis des Invalides, Paris, 1675–1706.   *B.* Sir Christopher Wren: St. Paul's Cathedral, London, 1675–1710.

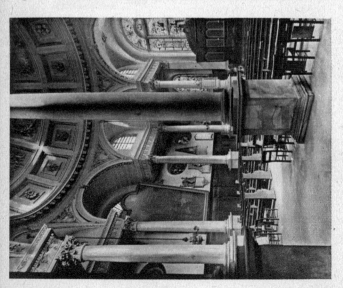

A. Sir Christopher Wren: St. Stephen's Walbrook, London, 1672–78.   B. Sir John Vanbrugh: Blenheim Palace, begun 1705.

A. Sir John Vanbrugh: gate pavilion of kitchen wing, Blenheim Palace. *B.* Robert Adam: gate screen, Syon House, 1773.

A. Blenheim from the air (Palace by Sir John Vanbrugh, grounds by Lancelot Brown). *B.* Robert Adam: Syon House, near London, the library, designed *c.* 1765.

Sir John Soane: design for his own house, Lincoln's Inn Fields, London, 1813. *B.* Friedrich Gilly: Plan for a National Theatre, Berlin, 1797–98.

A. Sir Robert Smirke: British Museum, London, begun 18
B. Sir Charles Barry and A. W. N. Pugin: Houses of Parliame
London, begun 1835.

A. Sir Charles Barry: Reform Club, London, begun 1837.
B. Charles Garnier: the Opera, Paris, 1861–74.

Walter Gropius: Model Factory, *Werkbund* Exhibition, Cologne, 1914.

the serene calm of a Lorraine landscape. The Rococo had to die, before this kind of beauty could be reproduced. The Leasowes, the garden which William Shenstone the poet had laid out for himself about 1745, was apparently amongst the first to replace the " twisting and twirling " of the earlier style by a gentler flow of curves which, together with the many memorial seats and temples which he erected, helped to rouse feelings of pleasant meditation. The great name in the history of mid-18th-century gardening is Lancelot Brown (Capability Brown, 1715–1783). His are the wide softly sweeping lawns, the artfully scattered clumps of trees and the serpentine lakes which revolutionised garden art all over Europe and America (pl. XLIV A). This is no longer Rococo, it has the gentle simplicity of Goldsmith's *Vicar of Wakefield* and the chaste elegance of Robert Adam's architecture.

But Adam's is a more complex case than Brown's. Robert Adam (1728–1792) is internationally known as the father of the Classical Revival in Britain. His revival of Roman stucco decoration and his delicate adaptation of classical motifs have influenced the Continent just as widely as the new English style in gardening. Yet delicacy is hardly what our present knowledge of Greece and Rome would lead us to expect from a true classical revivalist. Where in Adam's work is the severe nobility of Athens or the sturdy virility of Rome? There is in fact more severity in Lord Burlington's Palladianism and more virility in Vanbrugh than can anywhere be found in Adam. Compare, e.g., the walls of Adam's Long Gallery at Sion House (pl. XLIV B) with those of any Palladian mansion. Adam covers his walls with dainty and exquisitely executed stucco work in a light and quick rhythm. And he loves to run out a room into a gently rounded niche screened off by two free-standing columns with an entablature above. This veiling of spatial relations, this transparency—air floating from room to apse between the columns and above the entablature—is decidedly anti-Palladian, original and spirited. It occurs again in exterior architecture in the entrance screen to the grounds of Sion House (pl. XLIII B). Here too Lord Burlington would have spoken of flippancy and frippery. And Vanbrugh's centre pavilions in the wings of Blenheim Palace (pl. XLIII A) look, compared with Adam's screen, like boulders piled up by a giant. Adam's gracefully ornamented pilasters and the lion in profile silhouetted against the sky make Vanbrugh appear a tartar, Burlington a pedant. What Adam admired in a building is, in his own words: " the rise and fall, the advance and recess, and other diversity of forms ", and " a variety of light mouldings ".

Now this is eminently revealing. It is neither Baroque nor Palladian—although in the exteriors of his country houses Adam did not often depart from Palladian standards —nor is it classical. It is Rococo if anything—yet another passing and concealed appearance in England of the general European style of the mid-18th century. All the same, it is not wrong either to see in Robert Adam a representative of the Classical Revival. He did go to Rome as a young man, from there crossed over to Spalato to study and measure the remains of Diocletian's Palace, and after his return home published the results of his research as a sumptuous volume in 1763. Now these engraved folios of the monuments of antiquity are quite rightly regarded as a hall mark of the Classical Revival. Adam's was preceded by the most important of all, James Stuart's and Nicholas Revett's *Antiquities of Athens*, of which the first volume came out in 1762. The two architects had worked at the expense of the recently founded Society of Dilettanti, the London club of archeologically interested gentlemen. Six years later the temples of Paestum were illustrated by Thomas Major. In these books the architect and the virtuoso in England could see for the first time the strength and simplicity of the Greek Doric order. For what until then, and ever since the Books of Orders of the 16th century, had been known and used as Doric, was the much slenderer variety now known as Roman, if fluted, and Tuscan, if not fluted. The short and thick proportions of the Greek Doric order, and the complete absence of a base, shocked the Palladians. Sir William Chambers, champion of Palladian traditions in the generation after Burlington and one of the founders of the Royal Academy in 1768, called it downright barbaric. Adam did not like it either. Its reappearance in the books of the

sixties is memorable.   It became the *leitmotif* of the severest
phase or variety of the Classical Revival, that known in
England as the Greek Revival.   Stuart and Revett's work
was paralleled in French by Le Roi's skimpier *Ruines de
Grèce* of 1758 and in German by Winckelmann's classic
History of Ancient Art of 1763—the first book to recognise
and analyse the true qualities of Greek art, its " noble simplicity and tranquil greatness ".

However, Winckelmann's recognition of these qualities
was still more literary than visual; for he placed the Apollo
Belvedere and the Laocoon, that is examples of Late Greek
Baroque and Rococo, higher than any other antique
statuary.   Would the figures of Olympia and Aegina and
perhaps even those of the Parthenon have shocked him?   It
is not at all unlikely.   His Grecian taste probably did not
go further than say Josiah Wedgwood's.   Wedgwood copied
vases from those Greek examples of the 5th century which
were then believed to be Etruscan, and even called his new
factory up by Stoke-on-Trent Etruria.   But the style of
Wedgwood ware is gentle and elegant—an Adam not a
Greek style.   Still, there is the undeniable desire to be
Greek, the marked tendency in archeological publications to
prefer the Greek to the Roman, and there is, if not in Adam,
in his contemporary James Stuart, Athenian Stuart (1713–
1788), the actual copying in earnest of complete Greek
structures on Northern soil and the putting up of Doric
temples for Northern patrons.   If this is not a genuine Greek
Revival, what is?   But once again, if we forget about associations and intentions and simply use our eyes, we see
miniature pavilions in Doric forms placed into landscape
gardens—picturesque pieces of garden furnishing.   Such
a Doric temple of Stuart's, e.g., graces the grounds at Hagley
near Birmingham, and close to it the same owner put up at
the same time a Gothic ruin as a keeper's lodge and a rustic
seat to the memory of Thomson of the *Seasons*.

The only difference between the Doric and the Gothic of
Hagley is that the one is tolerably correct and the other is
not.   The owner, owing to his classical education watched
the one, but could not watch the other.   Architects too and
even country builders knew by 1760 enough of the orders

and the details of antiquity to be able to reproduce a Pantheon *en miniature* or a half-broken Roman aqueduct without too many blunders. But in the case of the earliest Gothic Revival antiquarian knowledge was still scanty. Thus while the result in the Greek and Roman copies tends to be somewhat dry, the innumerable Gothic seats, hermits' cells, " umbrellos " and sham ruins (fig. 56) are

Terminary Seat.

Fig. 56.—Garden Seat from P. Decker's *Gothic Architecture Decorated*, 1759.

charmingly naïve and lighthearted—a Gothic Rococo, as Adam's was a classical Rococo.

To Horace Walpole belongs the credit of having inspired and commissioned the first complete country house in the Gothic style: Strawberry Hill near London, begun in 1747. Walpole was ahead of his day in insisting on correct details, especially in his interiors, where fireplaces or wall panelling were copied from engravings after mediæval tombs and screens. He evidently admired other qualities in the Gothic

style than we do. In letters of 1748 and 1750 he talks of
" the charming venerable Gothic " and the " whimsical air
of novelty " which Gothic motifs give to contemporary
buildings. And charming and whimsical Strawberry Hill is
indeed with its thin, papery exterior work and the pretty
gallery inside whose gilt fan-vaults and tracery have mirrors
set in as panels. This playful use of Gothic forms is closer
in spirit to Chippendale's Chinese furniture than to Words-
worth's feelings at Tintern Abbey or to Victorian Neo-
Gothic churches. Walpole himself was against the fashion
of the *Chinoiserie*; but for a generalising view of the style
of 1750 a Chinese bridge, a minature Pantheon and a Gothic
ruin all belong together. In fact we find that even Robert
Adam enjoyed drawing ruins with all the Rococo sparkle of
Piranesi, and occasionally designed domestic work in a
mildly mediæval taste. And we also find Sir William
Chambers in spite of his staunch adherence to Palladianism
designing the Pagoda at Kew Gardens.

Kew had originally the most varied set of such Rococo
garden extravanganzas : besides the Pagoda (which alone
survives) a temple of Pan, a temple of Æolus, a temple of
Solitude, a temple of the Sun, a temple of Bellona, a temple
of Victory, a house of Confucius, a Corinthian colonnade,
an Alhambra, a Mosque, a Gothic Cathedral, a ruin, various
stone seats, etc. The fun of Turkish, Moorish, Gothic and
Chinese in this *omnium gatherum* of exotic styles is that of
Voltaire's *Zadig* and *Babouc* and of Montesquieu's *Lettres
Persanes*, that is one of a sophisticated Rococo double-
meaning. Not much of the solemn meditation of the
Romantics could in fact be evoked by a Pagoda. When the
Romantic Movement somewhat later instilled these senti-
ments into gardening, a good many of the current garden
adornments were eliminated as unsuitable. Yet to Walpole
too Strawberry Hill had associational qualities. It was, in
some ways, his *Castle of Otranto*. It seems difficult to
believe that; but that Beckford's mansion, Fonthill Abbey,
with its vast galleries and enormous spire had to him some
of the awe-inspiring qualities of the dark Middle Ages can
be appreciated from surviving illustrations. Here the
eccentricity of a millionaire seems to have created something

truly romantic.   Fonthill was built by James Wyatt (1746–1813) from 1796 onwards.   But already as early as 1772 Goethe in front of Strasbourg Cathedral had found words of passionate admiration for the Gothic spirit in architecture. " It rises like a most sublime, wide-arching Tree of God, who with a thousand boughs, a million of twigs, and leafage like the sands of the sea, tells forth to the neighbourhood the glory of the Lord, his master. . . . All is shape, down to the minutest fibril, all purposes to the whole.   How the firm-grounded gigantic building lightly rears itself into the air ! How filagree'd all of it, yet for eternity. . . .   Stop brother, and discern the deepest sense of truth . . . quickening out of strong, rough, German soul . . .   Be not girled, dear youth, for rough greatness by the soft doctrine of modern beauty-lisping."*

Now here the Gothic style is no longer something in the same category as Rococo, Chinese and Hindu, it stands for all that is genuine, sincere, elemental—in fact very much for what Winckelmann, and only a little later Goethe himself, saw in the art of Greece.   The Greek and the Gothic were both, in the minds of serious æstheticians and artists, the salvation from 18th-century flippancy.   But they could not be an effective remedy.   For no healthy style can stop at the mere imitation of another.   The Renaissance had not done it.   The Grecians of the early 19th century did it too often. Goethe in the most classical mood of his *Iphigenia* remained essentially original.   But in fact what he had praised more than anything at Strasbourg was originality in the sense of Young.   And so the few architects of Goethe's era who possessed true genius used the forms of Greece and Rome with the greatest freedom.   Of Greece and Rome ; for an equally free and masterly style based on Gothic principles time was not yet ripe.   The sense of mediæval building had not yet been sufficiently digested, to allow for a revival in another than an imitative sense.

Two architects above all others must be mentioned as the creators of an original idiom of 1800 : Sir John Soane in England and Friedrich Gilly in Prussia.   Soane (1753–

* Geoffrey Grigson's translation, published in *The Architectural Review*, vol. 99, 1946.

837) had gone through apprenticeship and Royal Academy uition, when he went to Rome in 1778. Already amongst is earliest designs there is an amazingly personal blend of Baroque grandeur of composition with Grecian severity of etail. Soane was the first (except for Piranesi, the engraver) to understand the *terribilità* of the Greek Doric rder. Then during the nineties Soane discovered that the everity which was his aim could be achieved by sheer unadorned surface—a discovery which makes his work appear o topical to-day. He had been appointed architect to the Bank of England in 1788.

The exterior, before it was converted by recent Governors and Directors into a podium for a piece of 20th-century commercial showiness, indicates this new and to the majority hocking austerity. The interiors, preserved though atrociously ill-treated, give an even clearer idea of his sense of surface integrity. Walls flow smoothly into vaults. Mouldings are reduced to a minimum. Arches sit on piers which hey seem to touch only in points. No precedent is allowed o cramp the master's style. The Dulwich Gallery of 1811–1814 (damaged by bombs but not irreparably) and Soane's own house in Lincoln's Inn Fields (pl. xlv A), built in 1812–13 and intended to be carried on to more than double its width, are his most independent designs. The ground floor of the house has severely plain arcading in front of the actual wall; the first floor repeats this unusual motif with the variation of a centre with Ionic columns supporting the thinnest of architraves, and wings where the weight of the piers is ightened by typically Soanian incised ornament. The top pavilions on the left and the right are equally original. Except for the Ionic columns there is not one motif in the whole façade that has a Greek or Roman ancestry. Here more than anywhere in architecture England approached a new style unhampered by the past, and a style moreover that possesses the crispness and precision of the dawning machine age. Soane for all we know was not in special sympathy with that age, which in most of its social and visual aspects was still sordid enough. Soane was a wilful, obstinate and irritable character, and wilful is his almost *Art Nouveau* looking ornament. But its meaning is clear. These delicate lines emphasise the planes into which they are cut, just as the lack of pediments on the flat roofs emphasise the cubic relations of such planes. From the beginning of his career Soane had been fascinated by this problem of cubic relations. He first expressed it with massive Doric columns and rustication, but later with flat surfaces of seeming skin or film or slab thinness.

The same faith in the bare surface but not the same elegance appears with a much more aggressive force in the work of a few French architects of the time of the Revolution. Claude Nicolas Ledoux (1736–1806) has only within the last fifteen years been rediscovered. He was an eccentric, cantankerous and quarrelsome. But his designs since

Fig. 57.—Claude-Nicolas Ledoux: One of the city gates of Paris, designed between 1784 and 1789.

1776 are amongst the most original ever conceived by any architect, original sometimes to the verge of mania: a completely spherical house, a pyramidal house, fantastic projects for vast community buildings. His planning is as boldly Baroque as Soane's. His predilection for the squat Doric column also connects him with Soane (fig. 57). He was no doubt influenced by England, and the publication of his work in 1804 may have influenced England in turn.

Friedrich Gilly (1772–1800), the Soane of Germany, was certainly inspired by Ledoux. He had his training at Berlin, one of a small group of young architects who about 1790 discovered the force of the true Doric order in Italy. Gilly himself however never saw Italy, and went to Paris and

London only after he had designed one of the two master-pieces which are left us to bear witness of his genius—left however only in drawings. Neither was ever carried out. The first is the National Monument to Frederick the Great (1797) the second a National Theatre for Berlin—clearly a conception of the Goethe age (pl. XLV B). The Doric portico without a pediment is a strong and grave opening. The semicircular windows, a favourite motif of the revolutionary architects of Paris, though imported from England, add strength to strength, and the contrast between the semi-cylinder of the auditorium walls and the cube of the stage is functionally eloquent and æsthetically superb. Here again we are close to a new style of the new century.

Why is it then that a hundred years had to pass before an original " modern " style was really accepted? How can it be that the 19th century forgot about Soane and Gilly and remained smugly satisfied with the imitation of the past? Such a lack of self-confidence is the last thing one would expect from an epoch so independent in commerce, industry and engineering. It is the things of the spirit in which the Victorian age lacked vigour and courage. Standards in architecture were the first to go; for while a poet and a painter can forget about their age and be great in the solitude of their study and studio, an architect cannot exist in opposi-tion to society. Now those to whom visual sensibility was given saw so much beauty destroyed all around by the sudden immense and uncontrolled growth of cities and factories that they despaired of their century and turned to a more inspiring past. Moreover the iron-master and mill-owner, as a rule self-made men of no education, felt no longer bound by one particular accepted taste as the gentleman had been who was brought up to believe in the rule of taste. It would have been bad manners to build against it. Hence the only slightly varied uniformity of the English 18th-century house. The new manufacturer had no manners, and he was a convinced individualist. If, for whatever reasons, he liked a style in architecture, then there was nothing to prevent him from having his way and getting a house or a factory or an office building or a club built in that style. And unfortunately for the immediate future of architecture he knew of a good many possible styles, because—as we have seen—some sophisticated and leisurely *cognoscenti* of the 18th century had explored for fun certain out-of-the-way architectural idioms, and a set of Romantic poets was revelling in nostalgic fantasies of the distant in time and space. The Rococo had reintroduced alien styles, the Romantic Movement had endowed them with sentimental associations. The 19th century lost the Rococo's lightness of touch and the Romantics' emotional fervour. But it stuck to variety of style, because associational values were the only values in architecture accessible to the new ruling class.

We have seen Vanbrugh's defence of ruins for associational reasons. Sir Joshua Reynolds in his thirteenth *Discourse* of 1786 made the same point more neatly. He explicitly counts amongst the principles of architecture " that of affecting the imagination by means of association of ideas. Thus," he continues, " we have naturally a veneration for antiquity; whatever building brings to our remembrance ancient customs and manners, such as the castles of the Barons of ancient Chivalry, is sure to give this delight."

Hence on the authority of the late President of the Royal Academy the manufacturer and merchant could feel justified in placing associational criteria foremost. Visual criteria his eyes were not trained to appreciate. But the eyes of architects were; and it was a grave symptom of a diseased century that architects were satisfied to be story-tellers instead of artists. But then painters were no better. They too, to be successful, had to tell stories or render objects from nature with scientific accuracy.

Thus by 1830 we find a most alarming social and æsthetic situation in architecture. Architects believed that anything created by the pre-industrial centuries must of necessity be better than anything made to express the character of their own era. Architects' clients had lost all æsthetic susceptibilities, and wanted other than æsthetic qualities to approve of a building. Associations they could understand. And one other quality they could also understand and even check: correctness of imitation. The free and fanciful treatment of styles developed into one of archeological exactitude. That this could happen was due to that general sharpening of the tools of historical knowledge which characterises the 19th century. It is in truth the century of Historicism. After the system-building 18th, the 19th substituted to an amazing extent the study, say, of existing philosophies to the study of metaphysics, ethics, æsthetics, etc., themselves. And so it was in theology and philology too. Similarly architectural scholarship abandoned æsthetic theory and concentrated on historical research. Thanks to a subdivision of labour which architecture as all other fields of art, letters and science took over from industry, architects were always able to draw from a well-assorted stock of historical detail. No wonder that little time and desire were left for the development of an original style of the 19th century. Even with regard to Soane and Gilly we have to be careful not to over-estimate their originality and " modernity ". Soane did a great deal that is more conventional than his own house. There are even some Gothic designs by him. And Gilly drew and published in detail the grandest of the mediæval castles of the German Knights in East Prussia. Exquisite as these drawings are, the attitude that made Gilly spend so much time on them is only partially romantic and patriotic. Antiquarian ambition is at least as conspicuous in these careful renderings of Gothic interiors. The case of Girtin's and Turner's early water colours is very similar. They are the transition (though still a romantic transition full of creative power) between the polite 18th-century engravings of Athens and Paestum and the voluminous 19th-century books on Cathedral Antiquities and mediæval details.

Amongst such books the transition can also be noted: the earliest are still rather sketchy, while later they became more and more thorough and as a rule rather dull. In actual buildings we find exactly the same development from the elegant and whimsical but sometimes inspired to the learned but sometimes deplorably pedestrian. Strawberry Hill stands for Rococo-Gothic, Robert Adam for a Rococo-Classical Revival. The next generation is characterised by John Nash (1752–1835). Nash had nothing of the intransigent creative fury of Soane. He was light-handed, careless, socially successful, and artistically conservative. His frontages of old Regent Street and most of his palace-like façades round Regent's Park, planned and carried out between 1811 and about 1825, are still of an 18th-century suppleness. What makes them memorable is the way in which they form part of a brilliant town-planning scheme, a scheme linking up the Picturesque of the 18th century with the Garden City ideas of the 20th. For these vast terraces face a landscape park, and a number of elegant villas are placed right in the park—the fulfilment of what had been foreshadowed in the juxtaposition of houses and lawn in the Royal Crescent at Bath. While the Regent Street–Regent's Park frontages are almost entirely classical, Nash built with the same gusto Gothic if required. He had a nice sense of associational propriety; as shown in his choice of the Neo-Classical for his town house and of the Gothic for his country mansion (complete with Gothic conservatory). Moreover he built Cronkhill in Shropshire (1802) as an Italianate villa with a round-arched loggia on slender columns and with the widely projecting eaves of the Southern farmhouse (Roscoe's *Lorenzo Medici* had come out in 1796), he built Blaise Castle near Bristol (1809) in a rustic Old-English cottage style with barge-boarded gables and thatched roofs (one is reminded of the *Vicar of Wakefield*, Marie Antoinette's dairy in the Park of Versailles, and Gainsborough's and Greuze's sweet peasant children), and he continued the Brighton Pavilion in a Hindu fashion, first introduced just after 1800 at Sezincote in the Cotswolds, where the owner, because of personal reminiscences, insisted on the style. " Indian Gothic " was the eminently characteristic contemporary name of the style.

So here, in the early years of the 19th century, the fancy-dress ball of architecture is in full swing: Classical, Gothic, Italianate, Old-English. By 1840 pattern-books for builders and clients include many more styles: Tudor, French Renaissance, Venetian Renaissance and others. That does not however mean that at all moments during the 19th century all these styles were really used. Favourites changed with fashion. Certain styles became associationally branded. A familiar example is the Moorish synagogue. Another is the perseverance of the battlemented castle for prisons. An account of architecture from 1820 to 1890 is bound to be one of the coming and going of period styles.

On the Classical side 1820–1840 is characterised by the most correct Neo-Greek. Fancy had left the treatment of antiquity even earlier than that of the Middle Ages. The results are competent, and in the hands of the best architects of a noble dignity. The British Museum, begun in 1824 by Sir Robert Smirke (1780–1867), is amongst the best examples in Britain (pl. XLVI A), or would be if its front with its grand

Fig. 58.—Carl Friedrich Schinkel: The Old Museum (Altes Museum), Berlin, 1822–30.

Ionic order of the Erechtheum in Athens could be seen from a distance; Carl Friedrich Schinkel (1781–1841), Gilly's pupil, is the greatest, most sensitive and most original representative on the Continent, William Strickland (1787–1854) probably the most vigorous in the United States.

For now, with the Greek Revival, America can no longer be left out of a picture of Western architecture. American building had been colonial to the end of the 18th century; colonial as the Latest Gothic, Renaissance and Baroque buildings of the Spanish and the Portuguese in North, Central and South America. The Greek Revival in the

United States is also still closely dependent on European, especially English examples, but national qualities, such as a remarkable stress on engineering technique, sanitary installation and equipment in general, now come to the fore. The ideological background of the strict Neo-Greek is the liberal humanism of the educated classes in the early 19th century, the spirit of Goethe, i.e., the spirit which created our first public museums and art galleries, and our first national theatres, and which is responsible for the reorganisation and the broadening of education.

On the Gothic side the corresponding development leads back to the Romantic Movement. Young Goethe's enthusiasm for Strasbourg had been a revolutionary genius's worship of genius. To the generation after his, the Middle Ages became the ideal of Christian civilisation. Friedrich Schlegel, one of the most brilliant of Romantic writers and one of the most inspired Gothicists, became a convert to the Roman Catholic church. That was in 1808. Châteaubriand had written his *Génie du Christianisme* in 1802. Then, about 1835 in England, Augustus Welby Pugin (1812-52) transferred the equation of Christianity and Gothic into architectural theory and practice. With him, to build in the forms of the Middle Ages is a moral duty. And he went further. He contended that, as the mediæval architect was an honest workman and a faithful Christian, and as mediæval architecture is good architecture, you must be an honest workman and a good Christian to be a good architect. In this the associational attitude appears fatefully extended. Similarly contemporary Classicists began to brand the architect who favoured Gothic as an obscurantist and, worse still, his work as popery. On the whole the arguments of the Gothicists proved stronger and had, in an unexpected way, a more beneficial effect on art and architecture, but the æsthetic value of the buildings designed by the Classicists was higher. The Houses of Parliament, begun in 1836, are æsthetically more successful than any later large-scale public building in the Gothic style (pl. XLVI B). The competition—a significant symptom—had demanded designs in the Gothic or Tudor style. A monument of national tradition had to be in a national style. The architect Sir Charles Barry

(1795–1860) preferred the Classical and the Italian. But Pugin worked with him and was responsible for nearly all the detail inside and outside. Hence the building possesses an intensity of life not to be found in other architects' endeavours in the Perpendicular style.

Yet even Pugin's Gothic turns out to be only a veneer, as soon as the Houses of Parliament are examined as a whole. They have, it is true, a picturesque asymmetry in their towers and spires, but the river front is, in spite of that, with its emphasised centre and corner pavilions a composition of Palladian formality. You can without much effort visualise it with porticoes of a William Kent or John Wood type. And strangely enough, the British Museum, perfectly Greek as it appears, reveals to the deeper-searching an equally Palladian structure. Centre portico and projecting wings are familiar features. The Athens of Pericles never conceived anything so loosely spread-out.

So while the battles raged between Goth and Pagan, neither realised how all this application of period detail remained on the surface. Moral arguments and associational tags were freely used, but architecture as a job of designing to fulfil functions remained unheeded—or at least undiscussed. Even to-day in such cases as the British Museum and the Houses of Parliament people think much too much of æsthetics and too little of function. Yet it should not be forgotten that to build a palace for democratic government and a palace for the instruction of the people was equally new. In fact to erect public buildings, specially designed as such, had been extremely rare before 1800. There were town-halls of course, and London had the Royal Exchange. Somerset House also had been intended for Government offices and learned societies from the beginning. But these were exceptions. If one takes the 19th century on the other hand, and tries to pick out the best examples of town architecture of all dates and all countries, a number of churches will have to be included, palaces rarely, private houses of course; but the vast majority of what one would collect are Governmental, municipal and later private office buildings, museums, galleries, libraries, universities and schools, theatres and concert halls, banks and exchanges, railway stations, department stores, hotels and hospitals, i.e., all buildings erected not for worship nor for luxury, but for the benefit and the daily use of the people, as represented by various groups of citizens. In this a new social function of architecture appears, representative of a new stratification of society. But the work in evolving plan forms for these new uses was more often than not anonymous, or at least appears so to us. The Renaissance library had been a hall of two or three aisles. The Renaissance hospital had been almost exactly identical in plan. Both came, without essential modifications, from the monastic buildings of the Middle Ages. Now schemes were worked out for separate library stores with stacking apparatus. For hospitals systems were tried of groups of separate wards in separate buildings for each kind of disease. For prisons the star-plan was invented (Pentonville) and accepted. For banks and exchanges the glass-covered centre hall or court proved the most serviceable solution. For museums and galleries a specially good system of lighting was essential, for office buildings the most flexible ground plan. And so every new type of building required its own treatment.

But the academician architects were too busy with new trimmings for façades to notice much of all that. When the struggle between Classicists and Gothicists began to subside, other styles took their place. In the mediæval field the generations before Pugin had been all for Perpendicular. To Pugin and those who followed him, notably Sir George Gilbert Scott, Perpendicular was anathema. Gothic had now to be of the 13th and early 14th century to be right, and Scott and his colleagues never minded replacing a genuine Perpendicular window by an imitation earlier one when they had to restore a church. In the camp of the Southerners the grand style of Italian Renaissance palazzi replaced the chastity of the Neo-Greek. Sir Charles Barry's Reform Club of 1837 in Pall Mall (pl. XLVII A) did much to popularise this fashion. It exhibits an increased desire for plasticity after the flatness of the Neo-Classical forms. On the Continent, Munich was the centre of this movement. The King of Bavaria liked it because of its association with the notion of the princely patron, the clubs of London because it reminded their members of an age of prosperous and cultured merchants. Then, in the forties and even more about the middle of the century, Elizabethan and Jacobean forms returned, and in France the French Renaissance of the 16th century. Their associational value was of course national; their æsthetic appeal lay in a still livelier play of ornament on surfaces. Apparently the underground tendency, covered up by changing period costumes, was towards the *mouvementé* and spectacular, the flamboyant style of Disraeli and the pompousness of Gladstone. Thus about 1850–60 Italianate forms became also more and more exuberant, until a Neo-Baroque was reached. Charles Garnier's Opera in Paris of 1861–74 is one of the earliest and best examples (pl. XLVII B). In England there is little of this *Second Empire* style. A revival of Palladianism in its most Baroque form took its place, and a strong inspiration from the Wren of Greenwich Hospital. Then with a slight sobering of form and a marked influence from a Classical Re-revival in America (McKim, Mead and White) a characteristically prosperous Edwardian Imperial style was arrived at (Selfridge's). In Germany the late 19th- and early 20th-century Neo-Baroque goes under the name of Wilhelmian; in Italy it has disgraced Rome with the national monument to King Victor Emmanuel II.

However, by the time these buildings were designed, a reaction had come and spread against so superficial—truly superficial—a conception of architecture. It did not originate with the architect. It could not; because it concerned problems of social reform and of engineering, and architects were not interested in these. Most of them loathed the industrial development of the age just as heartily as the painters. They did not see that the Industrial Revolution, while destroying an accepted order and an accepted standard of beauty, created opportunities for a new kind of beauty and order. It offered to the imaginative new materials and new manufacturing processes, and opened up a vista towards architectural planning on an undreamt-of scale.

As for new materials, iron, and after 1860, steel made it possible to achieve spans wider than ever before, to build higher than ever before, and develop ground plans more flexible than ever before. Glass, in conjunction with iron and steel, enabled the engineer to make whole roofs and whole walls transparent. Reinforced concrete introduced at the end of the century combines the tensile strength of steel with the crushing strength of stone. Architects knew little of these things. They left them to the engineers. For about 1800, in connection with the growing subdivision of competencies, the architect's and the engineer's had become different jobs for which a different training was provided. Architects learnt in the offices of older architects and in schools of architecture, until they set up in practice themselves doing what the civil-servant-architect had done in the 17th century, but now chiefly for private clients instead of the State. Engineers were trained in special university faculties or (in France and Central Europe) special technical universities. The most perfect examples of iron architecture, the suspension bridges such as Brunel's Clifton Bridge, designed in 1829–31 and begun in 1836, and the Eiffel Tower of 1889, are the work of engineers, not of architects. Paxton who conceived the Crystal Palace of 1851 was a landscape gardener used to the iron and glass work of conservatories. The men who introduced iron stanchions into the construction of American warehouses and occasionally, in the forties and fifties, opened whole fronts by glazing the whole interstices between the stanchions, are mostly unknown or undistinguished as architects.

In all this a fundamentally unsound conception of architecture as a social service is apparent. This was first recognised by Pugin who saw only one remedy: the return to the old faith of Rome. Then shortly after him, John Ruskin preached in *The Seven Lamps of Architecture* (1849) that a building must be truthful first of all. And a little later he began to realise that to achieve this, thought had to be given to social as well as æsthetic problems. The step from theory to practice was taken by William Morris (1834–96). He had undergone the influence of Ruskin and the Pre-Raphaelites, had actually been for a time a pupil of Rossetti, and also of one of the most conscientious Neo-Gothic architects. But he was not satisfied with either painting or architecture as he saw them practised, i.e., painting as the art of making easel pictures for exhibitions, and architecture as writing-desk and drawing-board work.

And whereas Ruskin kept his social activities apart from his æsthetic theory, Morris was the first to link up the two in the only way they could be successfully linked up. Instead of becoming a painter or an architect, he founded a firm for designing and making furniture, fabrics, wallpaper, carpets, stained glass, etc., and got his Pre-Raphaelite friends to join him. Not until the artist becomes a craftsman again, this was his belief, and the craftsman an artist, can art be saved from annihilation by the machine. Morris was a violent machine-hater. He attributed to mechanisation and sub-division of labour all the evils of the age. And from his point of view he was right. The solution he found was æsthetically sound, though socially not in the long run ade-quate. To build up a new style on design was sound, to try to build it up in opposition to the technical potentialities of the century was just as much escapism as the Classicist's disguising of a town hall as a Greek temple. The forms which Morris & Co. chose for their products were inspired by the late Middle Ages, as was Morris's poetry. But Morris did not imitate. He recognised Historicism as the danger it was. What he did was to steep himself in the atmosphere and the æsthetic principles of the Middle Ages, and then create something new with a similar flavour and on similar principles. This is why Morris fabrics and wall-papers will live long after all applied art of the generation before his will have lost its significance.

Morris's social-æsthetic theory as it was embodied in the many lectures and addresses he delivered from 1877 onwards will keep its life in history, too. By trying to revive the old faith in service, by indicting the contemporary architect's and artist's arrogant indifference to design for everyday needs, by discrediting any art created by individual genius for a small group of connoisseurs, and by forcing home with untiring zest the principle that art matters only " if all can share it ", he laid the foundation of the Modern Movement.

What Morris did for the philosophy of art and for design, R. Norman Shaw (1831–1912) did concurrently for the æsthetic approach to architecture.   His was a lighter touch, a quicker imagination, but a less discriminating taste.   In a professional career extending over more than forty years he never ceased to try the contemporary appeal of new period styles. He had no qualms about Historicism, as Morris had. His choice of examples from the past was dictated by a live sense of the picturesque, not by far-reaching principles as Morris's.   Thus he went in for half-timbered Tudor country houses, then for the many-gabled brick architecture of the Dutch Renaissance, then for a very restrained Neo-Queen Anne, or rather Neo-William and Mary, i.e., the style of the house illustrated (fig. 59), and finally joined in the pompous Edwardian Imperial.   He enjoyed however nothing more than mixing styles, and is at his best where he treats

Fig. 59.—Robert Norman Shaw: Stores and Inn at the Bedford Park Garden Suburb, Chiswick, 1878.

the past more freely (fig. 45).   By combining a few Tudor and a few 17th-century motifs with others of his own invention, he achieved a lightness and animation that makes Morris designs appear gloomy.   Norman Shaw was not quite the first to treat period styles so freely.   He was preceded in this by Morris's friend and collaborator Philip Webb (1831–1915).   The Red House which he designed for (and with) Morris in 1859 has already a combination (and a singularly successful one) of pointed arches with William and Mary windows.

But Norman Shaw's influence on the architectural profession was more immediate and more wide-spread than Webb's.   This is partly due to the fact that Shaw was an excellent teacher, too.   A generation of architects came from his studio to whom he left the freedom of following Morris's ideas, while following his own forms. They and some closer disciples of Morris founded the Arts and Crafts Movement. Once one knows what Morris taught, the name becomes self-explanatory. The most original interpretation of architectural traditions however came from a man not personally connected either with Shaw or with Morris, Charles F. Annesley Voysey (1857–1941). His designs for fabrics, wallpapers, furniture and metal work especially, so novel and so graceful, had an effect no less revolutionising than Morris's. In his buildings he appears just as fresh and lovable (fig. 60). Of period detail little is

Fig. 60.—Charles F. Annesley Voysey: House at Colwall, Malvern, 1897.

kept, but no effort is made to eliminate a general period flavour. In fact it is just the effortless, unaffected nature of Voysey's architecture that gives it its charm. Moreover, going more closely into it, one will be struck by the boldness of bare walls and long horizontal bands of windows. In such buildings of the 'nineties England came nearest to the idiom of the Modern Movement.

For the next forty years, the first forty of our century, no British name need here be mentioned. Britain had led Europe and America in architecture and design for a long time; now her ascendancy had come to an end. From Britain the art of landscape gardening had spread, and Adam's and Wedgwood's style, in Britain the Gothic

Revival had been conceived, to Britain the degradation of machine-produced applied art was due, to Britain the constructive reaction against it. The domestic revival of Morris, Norman Shaw and Voysey was British; British was the new social conception of a unified art under architectural guidance, and British the first achievements of design completely independent of the past. They are to be found in the work of Arthur H. Mackmurdo's Century Guild about 1885 and then in that of Voysey and some architects of the Arts and Crafts, above all Charles Rennie Mackintosh (1869–1928).

Art Nouveau, the first novel style on the Continent, and in fact a style, it seems now, desperately set on being novel, drew its inspiration from them. It started in Brussels in 1893 and had by 1895 become the *dernier cri* amongst the young artists and architects of Germany, Austria and France. Of Continental buildings designed between 1760 and the years of Art Nouveau not more than one or two have been mentioned in this chapter. All that was of importance either happened in Britain or could at least be followed just as easily in Britain as abroad. This statement need not be modified because Schinkel's in Berlin was the most perfect and progressive Greek Revival anywhere, or because Neo-Baroque never flourished in Britain as in France, or the appreciation of concrete in architecture came far earlier in France than in the other European countries.

But a few years before 1900 the position changed. The stage reached by Britain at that moment was one of truly contemporary design, but of a free traditionalism (as against the earlier more pedantic Historicism) in architecture. The step that had to be taken to recover a genuine, original style was that from Voysey's designs to a style in building equally bold. And the British character was (and is) all against such drastic steps, so uncompromising an attitude, so logical a procedure. Thus progress in Britain stopped for thirty years. Voysey's Tudor traditionalism was followed by a Wren and Georgian traditionalism, equally pleasant in domestic architecture, but feeble if not painfully inflated-looking in representational buildings.

The first private houses in which the new, original style of the 20th century can be recognised are Frank Lloyd Wright's (born 1869), built in the nineties in the neighbourhood of Chicago. They have the freely spreading ground plans, the interweaving of exteriors and interiors by means of terraces and cantilevered roofs, the opening up of one room into another, the predominant horizontals, the long window bands that are familiar in to-day's houses. Also at Chicago, and as early as the eighties and nineties, the first buildings were erected with steel skeletons (William Le Baron Jenney: Home Insurance Company 1884–85) and façades not disguising them (Holabird and Roche: Marquette Building 1894). As against this American priority in the appreciative use of steel, France was the first country to design houses of a genuine concrete character. They are of the first years of our century (Tony Garnier, born 1869; Auguste Perret, born 1873).

Then, between 1905 and 1914, Germany became the most important country. Here the liaison of design and architecture was most successful. Peter Behrens (1868–1938) designed factories and their products. The *Werkbund* was founded to be a meeting place of progressive manufacturers, architects and designers. And while in the United States and France the pioneers remained solitary, in Germany, twenty-five years ago, a style independent of the past had been accepted by quite a large public. In 1914, Walter Gropius (born 1883) showed the world, at an exhibition in Cologne, a factory so completely of to-day in every detail that it might be mis-dated by anybody (pl. XLVIII). It had a flat roof, again the general stress on horizontals, and two staircases entirely encased in curved glass so that the skeleton and the interior workings were proudly exposed. It will at once be recognised that in this motif as in the floating ground plan of Wright (and later on of Le Corbusier), and as incidentally also in the fantastic American highways intersections with wide areas given up to nothing but traffic bands on different levels, the eternal passion of the West for spatial movement once more expresses itself.

So by 1914 the leading architects of the younger generation had courageously broken with the past and accepted the machine-age in all its implications: new materials, new

processes, new forms, new problems. Of these the most
important is symbolised to an extent that probably future
civilisations will find as obscure as we find Avebury Circle
and the Kennet Avenue, by the American traffic crossings
just mentioned: namely the problem of modern town-
planning. It has been said before that one of the greatest
changes brought about by the Industrial Revolution was
the sudden growth of cities. To cope with this, architects
should have concentrated on the adequate housing of the
vast new working-class populations of these cities and on
the planning of adequate routes of traffic for the worker to
get to his job and back every day. But they were interested
in façades and nothing else; and so in a way were munici-
palities of the 19th century. New public buildings cropped
up everywhere. They were as splendid as money could buy
them. Take Manchester Town Hall, Glasgow University,
the Law Courts in Birmingham, London County Hall, or
take the series of magnificent but characteristically unrelated
monuments along the Ringstrasse in Vienna: the Gothic
Town Hall, the Classical Houses of Parliament, the Renaissance Museums, etc., or take the *Palais de Justice* in Brussels,
grander than any other—one cannot say that Governments
and city councils failed in their undeniable duty to give
representational architecture a chance.

Where they failed was in their infinitely greater duty to
provide decent living conditions for their citizens. One may
say that this was an outcome of the philosophy of liberalism,
which had taught them that everybody is happiest if left to
look after himself, and that interference with private life is
unnatural and always damaging; but while this explanation
will satisfy the historian, it could not satisfy the social
reformer. He saw that 95 per cent of the new houses in
industrial towns were put up by speculative builders as
cheaply as the scanty regulations would allow, and acted as
best he could. If he was a man like William Morris, he
preached a mediævalising socialism and escaped into the
happier world of handicraft. If he was like Prince Albert
and Lord Shaftesbury, he founded associations for improving by private generosity the dwellings of the artisan
and labourer. If however he was an enlightened employer

himself, he went one step further and commissioned an estate to be designed and built to a more satisfactory standard for his own workers. Thus Sir Titus Salt founded Saltaire near Leeds in 1853. It looks very drab now, but it was pioneer work. Lever Brothers began Port Sunlight in 1888 and Cadbury's Bournville in 1895. These two were the first factory estates planned as garden suburbs. From them—and Bedford Park near London which had been designed as early as 1875 by Norman Shaw on the same principle, though for private tenants of a wealthier class— the garden suburb and the garden city movement spread, another British contribution to the pre-history of modern European architecture.

Now in connection with this movement, architects re-entered the domain of town-planning. The greatest town-planning scheme between 1830 and 1880 had been the work of an administrative genius, Baron Haussmann, Napoleon III's prefect of the Seine department. His long, wide and straight roads all through the centre of Paris were drawn for the sake of civic magnificence and military security, but also for easier traffic to such focal points as railway stations. Haussmann was, however, not interested in housing, in the slums that developed behind his tall new façades, nor did he extend his appreciation of transport needs to the railways themselves.

But this problem, too, could not in the long run be neglected by the architect, once he accepted it as his job to design whole estates and suburbs. These new estates of small houses in their own gardens took a great deal of space. They were only possible right outside the built-over areas of towns. So the question of well-organised road and rail traffic became imperative. This question until then had been in the hands of the business man and again the engineer. Both had shown themselves staggeringly obtuse to architectural values. Some of the best vistas of London were cut into by railway bridges: the approach to St. Paul's, e.g., and the views down the Thames. Station buildings themselves, except for a few early ones such as old Euston and King's Cross, and except for the bewildering splendour of Gilbert Scott's Early English St. Pancras Station, were mean and untidy—at least in Britain. This unwillingness to accept the care for decent design as a public duty still applied quite universally to British big business and public services thirty years ago. The first to set an example of what immense improvements personal initiative can achieve was Frank Pick, to whom London owes a transport system beautifully designed from the station building down to the lighting standards and the litter baskets.

Frank Pick must be mentioned in a history of architecture as the prototype of the 20th-century patron. A Medici, a Louis XIV, are impossible in an age such as ours. The new Mæcenas is an administrator, a worker himself, with a house not much bigger than yours and mine, a cottage in the country, and a car far from spectacular. But as Managing Director of the London General Omnibus and the London Underground Companies, Pick saw that to assemble artists and architects round such a vast business enterprise would be to bring Morris's ideals up to date. So before the last war he began to reform the lettering used, had one of the best modern type-faces designed specially for his purpose and impressed it so deeply on the minds of millions that a revolution in British lettering ensued. Concurrently he started a campaign for better posters, and again succeeded in establishing Britain in the front rank of modern poster art. And when after the last war many new stations had to be built, he realised that the Continent had evolved a style more suited than contemporary English Neo-Georgian to express that synthesis of function and civic dignity that was his ideal. So he found the right architect in Mr. Charles Holden, and the London Underground stations (fig. 61) became the most perfect examples in London of the style of to-day, serviceable, uncompromisingly modern, and yet in keeping with the quiet distinction of the Georgian brick house.

Those who are doubtful about the blessings of the Modern Movement in architecture often say that the strongest argument against it is the very fact that its most representative examples are stations, factories, office buildings and the like. Now this is certainly not an accident. It would not be possible to find anything like the same number of good contemporary buildings for private luxury as for workaday se. But then, does not the architect today build for a population with nothing like the leisure for luxuries which patrons of the Baroque enjoyed? Must that not change the style, if it is a genuine style? Moreover, as has already been said, nearly every building that is designed nowadays serves masses and not individuals. Must not therefore our style be one adapted to mass production, not only in the sense of production in masses but also for masses?

Thus, if the new style is bare, if it goes straight to the point, there are good reasons for it. The ground had first of all to be cleared of the weeds of 19th-century sham ornamentation. Once that had been done, all available energy had to be devoted to research into function. What during the 19th

Fig. 61.—Charles Holden: Arnos Grove Station of the London Underground, 1932.

century had been done slowly and anonymously, now became the central task of the architect. If you have to build a soap factory, you must know how soap is being made. If your job is to design a nursery-school, you must find out all about nursery-school work. You cannot accept any plan on authority; it must be evolved anew every time from fundamentals. This Back-to-Fundamentals attitude with regard to function encouraged the same attitude to form. Again no authority was accepted, and again—after the first Art Nouveau flourish of unshackled imagination—the basic principles were rediscovered. This happened—a very hopeful sign—not only in architecture, but also in painting and sculpture. Cubism and then abstract art were the outcome, the most architectural art that had existed since the Middle Ages.   In architecture, sheer proportion at last took its legitimate place again.   No mouldings, no frills were permitted to detract one's attention from true architectural values: the relation of wall to window, solid to void, volume to space, block to block.   I need not here go into detail about the character of the new style, as it is the subject of a special volume in this series.*

The only fact that matters to the historian, and the one that he can state without falling into the rôle of counsel for the defence or for prosecution, is that the Modern Movement is a genuine and independent style.   This fact is full of promise.   For over a hundred years no style in that sense had existed.   As Western civilisation had become more and more subdivided, it had lost its faculty to create a language of its own.   An atomised society cannot have an architectural style.   Can we not take it then that the recovery of a true style in the visual arts, one in which once again building rules, and painting and sculpture serve, and one in which form is obviously representative of character, indicates the return of unity in society too?   Granted that this new style often looks rather forbidding and seems to lack human warmth.   But is not the same true of contemporary life?   Here, too, amenities to which we have been used are being replaced by something more exacting and more elementary.

Beyond stating this the historian should not go.   Whether the new social and architectural attitude heralds a last phase of Western civilisation or the dawn of a new, whether the style of the future will be at all similar to our own, and whether we shall like it—all this it is not for the historian to foretell.   His job is done when he has applied the principles of historical analysis as far into the problems of the present day as they can safely be applied.

* J. M. Richards: *An Introduction to Modern Architecture*, Pelican Books, 2nd edition, 1942.

BIBLIOGRAPHY

GENERAL

A. Michel: Histoire de l'Art, 18 vol., Paris, 1905–29.
Sir Banister Fletcher: A History of Architecture, 11th ed., London, 1943.
R. Sturgis: Dictionary of Architecture and Building, 3 vol., New York, 1901–2.
Talbot F. Hamlin: Architecture through the Ages, New York, 1941.
Fiske Kimball and G. H. Edgell: A History of Architecture, New York, 1918.
Wasmuths Lexikon der Baukunst, 5 vol., Berlin, 1929–37.
U. Thieme and F. Becker: Allgemeines Lexikon der bildenden Künstler, 32 vol., Leipzig, 1907 seqq.
M. S. Briggs: The Architect in History, Oxford, 1927.
G. Dehio and F. von Bezold: Die kirchliche Baukunst des Abendlandes, 10 vol., Stuttgart, 1884–1901.

BRITAIN

W. Godfrey: The Story of Architecture in England, 2 vol., London, 1928.
F. Gibberd: The Architecture of England from Norman Times to the Present Day, 5th ed., London, 1944.
N. Lloyd: A History of the English House, London, 1931.
H. Avray Tipping: English Homes, 9 vol., London, 1920–37.

FRANCE

C. Enlart: Manuel d'archéologie française, 2nd ed., 4 vol., Paris, 1919–32.
P. Lavedan: L'Architecture française, Paris, 1944.

GERMANY

G. Dehio: Geschichte der deutschen Kunst, 2nd ed., 6 vol., Berlin, 1921–31.

HOLLAND

F. Vermeulen: Handboek tot de Geschiedenis der Nederlandsche Bouwkunst, 3 vol., The Hague, 1928 seqq.
A. W. Weiszman: Geschiedenis der Nederlandsche Bouwkunst, Amsterdam, 1912.

ITALY

A. Venturi: Storia dell'Arte Italiana, 21 vol., Milan, 1901 seqq.
C. A. Cummings: A History of Italian Architecture, 2 vol., New York, 1901.

SPAIN

B. Bevan: A History of Spanish Architecture, London, 1938.
Marques de Lozoya: Historia del Arte hispanico, 4 vol., 1931–1945.

MIDDLE AGES

EARLY CHRISTIAN AND BYZANTINE

O. M. Dalton: East Christian Art, Oxford, 1925.
O. Wulff: Altchristliche und Byzantinische Kunst (Handbuch der Kunstwissenschaft), 2 vol., Neubabelsberg, 1914–18.
D. Talbot Rice: Byzantine Art, Oxford, 1935.
C. Diehl: Manuel d'Art Byzantin, 2nd ed., Paris, 1925–6.
L. Bréhier: L'Art Byzantin, Paris, 1924.

MEDIÆVAL GENERAL

W. R. Lethaby: Mediæval Art from the Peace of the Church to the Eve of the Renaissance, London, 1904.
A. Kingsley Porter: Mediæval Architecture, its origins and development, 2 vol., New York, 1909.
P. Frankl: Die Frühmittelalterliche und Romanische Baukunst (Handbuch der Kunstwissenschaft), Neubabelsberg, 1926.
A. W. Clapham: Romanesque Architecture in Western Europe, Oxford, 1936.
H. R. Hahnloser: Villard de Honnecourt, Vienna, 1935.

BRITAIN

F. Bond: An Introduction to English Church Architecture, 2 vol., London 1913.
C. E. Power: English Mediæval Architecture, 2nd ed., 3 vol., London, 1923.
E. S. Prior: A History of Gothic Art in England, London, 1900.
E. S. Prior: The Cathedral Builders in England, London, 1905.
T. F. Bumpus: The Cathedrals of England and Wales, London, 1905.
K. Escher: Englische Kathedralen, Zurich, 1929.
A. Hamilton Thompson: The Ground-Plan of the English Parish Church, Cambridge, 1911.
A. Hamilton Thompson: The Historical Growth of the English Parish Church, Cambridge, 1913.
J. C. Cox: The English Parish Church, London, 1914.
F. E. Howard: The Mediæval Styles of the English Parish Church, London, 1936.
A. Hamilton Thompson: Military Architecture in England during the Middle Ages, London, 1912.
G. Baldwin Brown: The Arts in Early England. Vol. 2: Anglo-Saxon Architecture, 2nd ed., London, 1925.
A. W. Clapham: English Romanesque Architecture, 2 vol., Oxford, 1930–4.
S. Gardner: A Guide to English Gothic Architecture, Cambridge, 1922.
J. Bilson: Les origines de l'architecture gothique, and Les premières croisées d'ogives en Angleterre, Revue de l'Art Chrétien, 1901 and 1902.
C. Enlart: Du Rôle de l'Angleterre dans l'Evolution de l'Art Gothique, Paris, 1908.

FRANCE

R. de Lasteyrie: L'Architecture Réligieuse en France à l'Époque Romane, 2nd ed., Paris, 1929.

J. Baum: Romanesque Architecture in France, 2nd ed., London, 1928.

C. Martin: L'Art Roman en France, 3 vol., Paris, c. 1910–14.

J. Evans: The Romanesque Architecture of the Order of Cluny, Cambridge, 1938.

E. Gall: Die Gotische Baukunst in Frankreich und Deutschland, vol. 1, Leipzig, 1925.

R. de Lasteyrie: L'Architecture Réligieuse en France á l'Époque Gothique, 2 vol., Paris, 1926–7.

C. Martin and C. Enlart: L'Art Gothique en France, 2 vol., Paris, c. 1913–25.

E. Mâle: L'Art Réligieux du XIIe Siècle en France, Paris, 1922.

E. Mâle: L'Art Réligieux du XIIIe Siècle en France, Paris, 1902 (English translation, 1913).

ITALY

C. Ricci: Romanesque Architecture in Italy, London, 1925.

C. Martin and C. Enlart: L'Art Roman en Italie, 2 vol., Paris, c. 1911–24.

A. Kingsley Porter: Lombard Architecture, 4 vol., Newhaven, 1915–17.

G. T. Rivoira: Lombardic Architecture, 2nd ed., Oxford, 1934.

W. Paatz: Werden und Wesen der Trecento-Architektur in Toskana, Burg, 1937.

SPAIN

V. Lampérez y Romea: Historia de la Arquitectura Cristiana Española en la Edad Media, 2nd ed., Madrid, 1930.

G. G. King: Pre-Romanesque Churches of Spain, Bryn Mawr, 1924.

A. S. Frischauer: Altspanischer Kirchenbau, Berlin and Leipzig, 1930.

G. E. Street (revised by G. G. King). Some Account of Gothic Architecture in Spain, London, 1914.

E. Lambert: L'Art Gothique en Espagne, Paris, 1931.

RENAISSANCE, MANNERISM AND BAROQUE IN ITALY

J. Burckhardt: Geschichte der Renaissance in Italien, 5th ed., Esslingen, 1912.

W. J. Anderson and A. Stratton: The Architecture of the Renaissance in Italy, London, 1927.

C. von Stegmann and H. von Geymüller: Die Architektur der Renaissance in Toskana, 12 vol., Munich, 1909.

A. Haupt: Renaissance Palaces of Northern Italy and Tuscany, London, c. 1931.

D. Frey: Architettura della Rinascenza, Rome, 1924.

J. Baum: Baukunst und Dekorative Plastik der Frührenaissance in Italien, Stuttgart, 1920.

C. Ricci: Baukunst der Hoch- und Spätrenaissance in Italien, Stuttgart, 1923.

G. Giovannoni: Saggi sull'Architettura del Rinascimento, Milan, 1931.

N. Pevsner: The Architecture of Mannerism, The Mint, 1945.

N. Pevsner: Gegenreformation und Manierisums, Repertorium für Kunstwissenschaft, vol. 46, 1925.
C. Gurlitt: Geschichte des Barockstils in Italien, Esslingen, 1887.
A. E. Brinckmann: Die Baukunst des 17 and 18 Jahrhunderts in den Romanischen Ländern (Handbuch der Kunstwissenschaft), Neubabelsberg, 1919 seqq.
C. Ricci: Baroque Architecture and Sculpture in Italy, London, 1912.
T. H. Fokker: Roman Baroque Art, 2 vol., Oxford, 1938.
Brunelleschi: H. Folnesics, Vienna, 1915.
Alberti: R. Wittkower, Journal of the Warburg and Courtauld Institutes, vol. 4, 1941.
Bramante: H. von Geymuller: Les Projets Primitifs pour la Basilique de St. Pierre à Rome, Vienna and Paris, 1875–80.
Raphael: T. Hofmann, 4 vol., Zittau, 1900–14.
Michelangelo: J. A. Symonds, 2 vol., London, 1893.
H. Thode: Kritische Untersuchungen, 6 vol., Berlin, 1902–13.
Michelangelo's Laurenziana Library: R. Wittkower, The Art Bulletin, vol. 16, 1934.
Giulio Romano: E. Gombrich, Jahrbuch der Kunsthistorischen Sammlungen in Wien, N.F., vols. 8 and 9, 1935–1936.
Serlio: W. B. Dinsmoor, The Art Bulletin, vol., 24, 1942.
Palladio: Sir Banister Fletcher, London, 1902.
F. Burger: Die Villen des Andrea Palladio, Leipzig, c. 1909.
Bernini: S. Fraschetti, Milan, 1900.
Borromini: E. Hempel, Vienna, 1924.

16TH TO 18TH CENTURY IN BRITAIN, FRANCE, GERMANY AND SPAIN

BRITAIN

T. Garner and A. Stratton: Domestic Architecture of England during the Tudor Period, 2nd ed., 2 vol., London, 1929.
J. A. Gotch: Early Renaissance Architecture in England, London, 1914.
J. A. Gotch: The English House from Charles I to George IV, London, 1918.
S. E. Rasmussen: London, the Unique City, London, 1937.
Inigo Jones: J. A. Gotch, London, 1928.
Wren: G. Webb, London, 1937.
    L. Weaver, London, 1923.
    Wren Society, 20 vol., London, 1924–44.
    Bicentenary Memorial Volume, published by the Royal Institute of British Architects, London, 1923.
Wood: M. A. Green, Bath, 1914.
Adam: J. Swarbrick, London, 1915.
    A. T. Bolton, 2 vol., London, 1922.

FRANCE

Sir Reginald Blomfield: A History of French Architecture, 1494–1774, 4 vol., London, 1911–21.
A. E. Brinckmann: Die Baukunst des 17 und 18 Jahrhunderts in den Romanischen Landern (Handbuch der Kunstwissenschaft), Neubabelsberg, 1919 seqq.

C. Martin: La Renaissance en France, 2 vol., Paris, c. 1910–12.
H. Rose: Spätbarock, Munich, 1922.
L. Hautecœur: Les Grands Palais de France, Le Louvre et les Tuileries, Paris, c. 1924.
L. Hautecœur: L'Histoire des Châteaux du Louvre et des Tuileries . . ., Paris and Brussels, 1927.
G. Brière: Le Château de Versailles, 2 vol., Paris, 2c. 1910.
J. Vacquier and Jarry: Les Vieux Hôtels de Paris, 22 portfolios, Paris, 1910–34.
A. Blunt: François Mansart, London, 1941.

GERMANY

W. Pinder: Deutscher Barock, 2nd ed., Königstein, 1924.
S. Sitwell: German Baroque Art, London, 1927.
M. Hauttmann: Geschichte der kirchlichen Baukunst in Bayern, Schwaben und Franken, 1550–1780, Munich, 1924.

SPAIN

A. Byne and M. Stapley: Spanish Architecture of the Sixteenth Century, New York, 1917.
O. Schubert: Geschichte des Barocks in Spanien, Esslingen, 1908.

19TH AND 20TH CENTURIES:

S. Giedion: Spätbarocker und Romantischer Klassizismus, Munich, 1922.
C. Hussey: The Picturesque, London, 1927.
N. Pevsner: The Genesis of the Picturesque, The Architectural Review, vol. 96, 1944.
Sir Kenneth Clark: The Gothic Revival, London, 1928.
N. Pevsner: Pioneers of the Modern Movement, from William Morris to Walter Gropius, London, 1936.
S. Giedion: Space, Time and Architecture, Harvard, 1941.
T. E. Tallmadge: The Story of Architecture in America, London, 1928.
J. M. Richards: An Introduction to Modern Architecture, Pelican Books, 2nd ed., 1942.
Soane: A. T. Bolton, London, 1927.
Nash: J. Summerson, London, 1935.
Gilly: A. Oncken, Berlin, 1935.
William Morris: J. W. Mackail, 2nd ed., London, 1922.
 A. Vallance, London, 1897.

SOME TECHNICAL TERMS EXPLAINED

Only less familiar architectural terms are included, and only those which have not already been explained in the places where they first occurred in the text.

Ambulatory: Aisle round an apse or a circular building.

Arcade: Group of arches on columns or pillars.

Architrave: Cf. 3 on page 227 A.

Attic: Low story above main cornice.

Basilica: Church with aisles and a nave higher than the aisles.

Bay: Vertical unit of a wall or façade; also compartments into which a nave is divided.

Caryatid: Sculptured figure used as a support.

Clerestory: Upper part of church nave with windows above the roofs of the aisles.

Cornice: Cf. 3 on page 229 F.

Cross: Cf. Greek cross.

Cross Rib: Cf. 1 on page 229 E.

Drum: Cf. 1 on page 227 B.

Entablature: Cf. 5 on page 227 A.

Greek Cross: Cross with all four arms of equal length.

Jamb: Cf. 1 on page 228 C.

Lantern: Cf. 2 on page 227 B.

Lierne: Cf. 5 on page 229 E.

Metope: Cf. 1 on page 227 A.

Mullion: Vertical division of a window.

Narthex: Porch in front of the nave and aisles of a mediæval church.

Ogee Arch: Cf. page 228 D.

Pediment: Cf. 1 on page 229 F.

Plinth: Projecting base of a building or a column.

Quoins: Cf. 2 on page 229 F.

Rustication: Wall treatment with large freestone blocks, either smooth with recessed joints, or with a rough, rock-like surface and recessed joints.

Solar: Chamber on an upper floor.

Spandrel: Cf. 6 on page 227 A.

String-course: Cf. 4 on page 229 F.

Tierceron: Cf. 4 on page 229 E.

Transom: Horizontal division of a window.

Transverse Rib: Cf. 2 on page 229 E.

Triglyph: Cf. 2 on page 227 A.

Voussoir: Cf. 2 on page 228 C.

A. Classical details.

1. Metope. 3. Architrave. 5. Entablature.
2. Triglyph. 4. Cornice. 6. Spandrel.

B. Dome

1. Drum. 2. Lantern.

227

C. Gothic Porch.

1. Jamb.   2. Voussoir.

D. Ogee Arch.

E. Gothic Vault.

| 1. Cross Rib. | 3. Ridge Rib. | 5. Lierne. |
| 2. Transverse Rib. | 4. Tierceron. | |

F. Queen Anne House.

1. Pediment.　　2. Quoins.　　3. Cornice.　　4. String-course.

INDEX

An Introduction to Modern Architecture A61

by J. M. RICHARDS

THIS BOOK sets out to explain what "modern" architecture is all about and how it has developed to its present stage. The author, not wishing it to appear as a professional mystery or merely a matter of correct taste, asks (and tries to answer) the simple question: "Conventions and habits apart, what sort of architecture do people really require?"

With the help of 44 gravure illustrations and numerous line drawings, he explains how modern buildings come to look as they do, discussing the technical practices and the changing needs and ideals on which modern architects' work is based. Also, believing that architecture can only be explained as part of a continuous growth, and realising therefore how essential it is to show modern architecture against the background out of which it grew, he has given one section of the book to an outline history of the struggle to produce a sane architecture which has been going on throughout the past hundred years.

Some Press Opinions

"One of the best general introductions to modern architecture on the market—and by far the cheapest. It should do much to provide modern architecture with its principal condition of success—a wide and understanding public."—*The Listener*.

"Sensible, thoughtful, and sensitive. People who buy this book are getting incalculable value. It is simple in expression and very easy to read; there could not be a better introduction to the subject."—*Building*.

"A cheaply acquired means for anyone to obtain the basis of understanding and enthusiasm to enable him to play his part as a layman in getting the buildings our post-war civilisation will need, even if it does not deserve them."—*Fortnightly Review*.

A PELICAN BOOK

THREE BOOKS OF KINDRED INTEREST

The Englishman Builds

by RALPH TUBBS

Member of the R.I.B.A. Reconstruction Committee and of the Council
of the Architectural Association.

The story, in text and picture, of the development of
domestic and public building in England through the
centuries.

Village Planning

by THOMAS SHARP

The English village has long occupied a central place in
the affections and pride of the people, countrymen and
townsmen alike. One of the problems of post-War
development is how to reconcile the preservation of all
that is best in this tradition with the requirements of the
new age. In text and picture, Mr. Sharp here shows
how the problem can be and is being tackled.

America Needed Houses

by HUGH CASSON, M.A., R.I.B.A.

An illustrated account of the housing achievement of the
U.S.A. 1940–1945.

Pelican Books